READING SKILLS
A Guide for Better Reading

READING SKILLS
A Guide for Better Reading

W. ROYCE ADAMS

Santa Barbara City College
Santa Barbara, California

JOHN WILEY & SONS, New York • Chichester • Brisbane • Toronto

Editors: Judy Wilson and Irene Brownstone
Production Manager: Ken Burke
Editorial Supervisor: Winn Kalmon
Composition and Make-up: Winn Kalmon

Library of Congress Cataloging in Publication Data

Adams, W. Royce
    Reading skills: a guide for better reading.

    (Wiley self-teaching guides)
    1. Reading--Programmed instruction.
LB1050.A26   428'.4'3   73-21849
ISBN 0-471-00780-3

Printed in the United States of America

10 9 8 7 6 5 4

Preface

Like most learned skills, reading requires practice. Unfortunately, many readers never receive enough practice in reading skills for them to reach their real potential. The purpose of this book is to provide self-teaching assistance to those who wish to develop their reading skills. Organized in a programmed fashion, the text contains exercises in reading paragraphs, articles from magazines and journals, newspaper articles, and textbooks. More specifically, the exercises provide practice in recognizing main ideas, supporting details, writing patterns and organization, distinguishing fact from opinion, and drawing inferences. In addition, the book provides methods and practice in vocabulary development, skim reading, scanning, and study reading procedures based on the SQ3R method developed by Francis Robinson.

The tasks included in this Self-Teaching Guide are not particularly unique for a reading textbook. What is unique is the approach it takes by allowing the student to work only in those areas of special need or reading concerns. The contents are also very practical and straightforward in approach. In addition, the contents have been used and tested with excellent results in the Learning Resources Center at Santa Barbara City College. Hopefully, the book will help many more students and general readers improve their reading skills.

Santa Barbara, California   W. Royce Adams
February 1974

Sources of reading selections (listed by pages on which they appear):

45-49   "Comprehension Skills" by Olive Niles, The Reading Teacher, September 1963. Reprinted by permission of the author and the International Reading Association, Newark, Delaware.

74   "White House doctor praises acupuncture." Reprinted by permission of United Press International.

77   "Noise isn't always something you hear." Reprinted by permission of the Santa Barbara News-Press, Santa Barbara, California.

80   "Gadget nets thieves $500,000 in metals." Reprinted by permission of United Press International.

84-87   "The Sugar Story" by Fred Rohe. Reprinted by permission of the author.

89-93   "Houseboating" by Jack Lind, Mainliner, August 1972. Reprinted by permission of United Air Lines, Chicago, Illinois.

97   page 839 from European Civilization Since the Middle Ages (second edition) by Edward R. Tannenbaum. New York: John Wiley & Sons, Inc., 1971. Reprinted by permission of the publisher.

117-119 "Hot Dog!," Sojourn Magazine, Vol. 1, no. 4. Reprinted by permission of the publisher.

126-131 "Motorcycling Gains New Image," Holiday Inn Magazine, May/June 1973. Reprinted by permission of the publisher.

137-139 "Easy Rider" by Steve Goldstein, Travel & Leisure Magazine, April/May 1973. Reprinted by permission of the author and American Express Publishing Corporation, New York, N. Y.

143-145 "Requirements: Aid or Deterrent to Education?" by Orvel E. Hooker. Reprinted by permission of City News Publishing Co., Southold, N. Y.

157-163 "Critical Reading—As If There's Any Other Kind" by Brother William J. Quaintance, The Reading Teacher, October 1966. Reprinted by permission of the author and the International Reading Association, Newark, Delaware.

167-172 "The Ambiguous American" (Part One) by Henry Steele Commager, New York Times Magazine, May 3, 1964. Copyright ©️ 1964 by the New York Times Company. Reprinted by permission.

191, 192-198, 217 from Psychology for a Changing World by Idella M. Evans and Patricia A. Smith. New York: John Wiley & Sons, inc., 1970. Reprinted by permission of the publisher.

Contents

READING SKILLS
A Guide for Better Reading

How to Read This Book

(1)   The phrase "reading between the lines" is a figure of speech usually referring to the ability to draw inferences; that is, the ability to understand what an author means when he isn't coming right out and saying it. In this book, however, you are literally going to read between the lines because it is a programmed book. That means that the material is presented in small units called frames.

Lines separate each frame. This is frame **(1)**. Go to frame **(2)**.

---

(2)   Here you are in frame **(2)**. Easy enough, right? Well, it can become confusing if you don't pay careful attention to which frame you are directed to read. Sometimes you may be told to skip a frame or two. The reason for this is that you may not need to read each frame, depending on how well and how fast you understand new concepts.

Now go to **(4)**.

---

(3)   There, see! You were told it wasn't always easy. You were directed to frame **(4)** and here you are in **(3)**. Yield not to temptation. Go to **(4)**.

---

(4)   You are now in frame **(4)** where you should be. Keep in mind that you must always go to the frame indicated or you may be getting answers to a wrong exercise or becoming involved in a new concept before you are ready.

(continued)

Go to ⑥.

---

⑤ Whoops, you did it again! Maybe you're just naturally curious?
Go to ⑥.

---

⑥ Check the statement below which best fits you.

1. I only bought this book because it was
required for a class.　　　　　　　☐ Go to ⑦.

2. I bought this book because it looked like
it might help me read better.　　　☐ Go to ⑧.

3. My mother gave me this book because
she's trying to tell me something.　☐ Go to ⑨.

---

⑦ If you only bought this book because it was required for a class,
you may not have the proper attitude toward it. In fact, you may
even resent the book because you spent money you'd rather have
used on other things. Hopefully, your attitude will change once you
get into this book. It can help you become a better reader which in
turn will help you become a better student, a better person, a better
parent, a better grandparent, a better great-grandparent, or whatever.

You say you bought the book because it was required for a class.
That means you are a student. Most students are given heavy reading assignments from a variety of sources. If you expect to do well,
you will need to develop reading skills to your fullest potential.

Go to ⑩ and see what you will get for your money's worth.

---

⑧ Good. That means you are already motivated to learn more about
reading and your reading ability. You don't need a "pep talk" on how

important it is to read better, so go to ⑩ where you can see what
this book will help you learn.

---

(9)   Well, your mother's a smart woman. She knows what's good for you. You've gotten this far with her help, so why stop now? Go to (10) where you can see what a wise mother you have.

---

(10)   By now you can see how this book is structured. You do not need to read every frame, only the ones which pertain to you and your needs.

This book is for readers who already read but do not read as well as they need or as well as they could with a little more practice. Reading is a skill and like any skill—playing golf, shooting archery, operating a lathe, changing the valves in an engine, or lifting weights —the more practice you get, the better you get. That, of course, depends on the right kind of practice.

When you finish this book, you will be able to:

> Read with better comprehension.
>
> Read with faster comprehension.
>
> Improve your vocabulary by establishing one or more of the vocabulary methods described in this book.
>
> Skim with better comprehension.
>
> Scan with greater accuracy.
>
> Read, understand, and remember textbook reading assignments by using the SQ3R method.

Now you know how to use this book and what it can do to help you read better. Choose one of the approaches listed below and get to work.

1.   Go to the Contents page and select the chapter you want to work in first.

2.   Go to Chapter 1, frame (1) and begin working through the book in a progressive fashion. If you have read STUDY SKILLS: A STUDENT'S GUIDE FOR SURVIVAL, another Wiley Self-Teaching Guide, co-authored with Robert Carman, you may already be familiar with some of the material in Chapters 1 and 4. Here we will go into more depth with more examples, so hang in there and learn.

CHAPTER ONE
Improving Comprehension

GOALS AND OBJECTIVES

General Goals: When you complete this chapter you will be able to:

(1) Establish a reading purpose that helps you get involved in the reading assignment.

(2) Remember better what you read.

(3) Recognize the difference between main ideas and supporting details.

(4) Recognize relationships in writing.

(5) Read more critically.

(6) Apply a systematic approach to vocabulary development.

Specific Objectives: When you complete this chapter you will be able to:

(1) Establish an identifiable purpose for every reading assignment.

(2) Distinguish among reading for pleasure, reading for practical application, reading for general ideas, reading to locate specific information, and reading to critically evaluate.

(3) Recognize the difference between main ideas and supporting details in expository reading.

(4) Recognize writing patterns, such as an author's use of examples, comparison or contrast, definition, explanation, or combination of patterns.

(5) Compare your average reading speed of comprehension with that of other students.

(6) Adopt a systematic approach for improving your vocabulary.

IMPROVING COMPREHENSION

Before you settle down to read this, find two pencils or one pencil and a pen and then resume your reading. We'll be here when you get back.

Do you have them? Good. Now, place a pencil between your lips. Don't bite it with your teeth. Just hold the pencil gently with your lips. Keep it there until you are directed to remove it.

Now, with another pencil or a pen, check those items which pertain to you or which you don't understand.

- [ ] 1. You usually read only when you have to.
- [ ] 2. You generally read everything—newspapers, poems, short stories, textbooks, novels—the same way and at the same speed.
- [ ] 3. You generally have trouble remembering what you read.
- [ ] 4. You have difficulty recognizing the difference between main ideas and supporting details.
- [ ] 5. You generally have trouble understanding relationships. (If you don't understand what we mean, check the box.)
- [ ] 6. You have trouble understanding an author's purpose and reading critically.
- [ ] 7. The pencil between your lips has been moving or falling from your mouth as you have been reading this.
- [ ] 8. You need help developing your vocabulary.

You may remove the pencil from your lips now. If you failed to follow directions, you may have to pry it from your teeth. Wipe off the pencil and go to frame (1).

---

(1)   If you did not check any of the items above, skip this chapter entirely. You don't need any help from it. Go to Chapter 2. If you did check any items, go to Frame 2.

---

(2)   If you checked item 1 or 2 or both, go to (8) now; otherwise, go on to (3).

---

(3)   If you checked item 3 or 4 or both, go to (30) now; otherwise, go to (4).

(4)   If you checked item 5, go to (45) now; otherwise, go on to (5).

(5)   If you checked item 6, go to (59) now; otherwise, go on to (6).

(6)   If you checked item 7, go to (46) now; otherwise, go on to (7).

(7)   If you checked item 8, go to (69) now; otherwise, go to (75).

(8)   If you are here, you checked item 1 or 2 or both. Checking those particular items indicates that you probably read everything with the same approach rather than letting your purpose for reading guide you. For instance, when a guy receives a letter from his gal, he's going to read that letter a lot differently than he is a chapter from a biology book. For one thing, he's more interested in the content of the letter, right? He can relate to that letter much better than a chapter on molecular theory. He wants, desires, craves to read the letter. He will probably read it several times, particularly the parts that say "I love you" or "I miss you" or "You are my Mr. Wonderful." His purpose for reading is to look for everything in that letter that reveals all is well between him and his girl. Can you imagine this guy's mind wandering off to something else while reading his letter? Can you imagine his forgetting what the letter says? Can you imagine his failing a test on the content of the letter? Now why isn't the desire to read a chapter on protein molecules or mitosis or the migration of lemmings just as strong and meaningful?

Most teachers wish they could make their required readings as interesting as a personal love letter. But since the desire to read study material generally isn't as strong (there probably are a few people who are in love with molecules and such, but that's another story), there is often a need to create a purpose for reading that is meaningful to you. When a teacher says, "Read Chapters Five and Six by Friday and be ready for a quiz," the assignment itself is no purpose. Sure, your purpose for reading will be to pass the quiz and the course, but you also need a purpose that is meaningful to you—just like the guy with the love letter.

(continued)

You need to establish a purpose that helps you get involved in the reading assignment.

The following frames discuss different types of purposes.

---

(9)   Purpose #1: Reading for Pleasure

One purpose for reading is strictly for pleasure. Which of the following materials do you think are read primarily with the purpose of pleasure? Check one.

a recipe for a cake   ☐ See (10)

MAD magazine   ☐ See (11)

an assigned chapter from a biology text   ☐ See (12)

---

(10)   If you read recipes for pleasure, you're as unusual as the guy who reads about molecules for pleasure. Most people read recipes with the purpose of using or applying the information they read. There may be pleasure in eating the cake, but not too much in reading about it.

Return to (9) and try another answer.

---

(11)   Right. While it's true that MAD Magazine could be assigned reading for some classes, usually the main purpose for reading material such as MAD is pleasure.

Go on now to (13) .

---

(12)   Very doubtful. Most textbook reading is not done with pleasure as its purpose. It might turn out to be interesting or even pleasurable, but the purpose for reading a textbook will not be to receive pleasure, but rather knowledge.

Return to (9) and try another answer.

---

(13)   Purpose #2: Reading for Practical Application

Another purpose for reading is to gain information which you can apply to or use in a particular situation. Which of the following materials do you think are read primarily for the purpose of practical application? Check one.

a newspaper editorial	☐	See ⑭
a personal love letter	☐	See ⑮
a recipe in a cookbook	☐	See ⑯

---

⑭   Probably not. A newspaper editorial is going to praise or judge someone, take a stand on some political or economic issue, or try to convince the reader to think a certain way. You may gain information that will help you decide how to vote on an issue, but that's not what Purpose #2 means. When you read directions in order to put a model airplane together, or you read a shop manual to learn how to run a piece of equipment, you are reading with the purpose of gaining information which you can apply or use.

Return to ⑬ and try another answer.

---

⑮   You're kidding! Well, maybe you're not. If the love letter says, "Yes, I'll marry you," information is being gained for practical application. However, we're discussing purposes for reading, and you don't read a love letter with the primary purpose of gaining usable information—not like you do a road map, the movie timetable, or TV program guides. These things are read so that you can apply or use what you learn from reading.

Return to ⑬ and select another answer.

---

⑯   Good choice. The purpose for reading a recipe is to use the information, to apply it in some way. Shop manuals, laboratory manuals, dress patterns, and bartender guides are all materials generally read with the purpose of practical application.

Go on to ⑰ .

---

⑰   Purpose #3: Reading for General Ideas

It is not always necessary to read every word on a page. If your purpose for reading is to get a general idea of the material being read, then you can read at faster speeds, skipping sections and looking only for main ideas, reading bold print headings and sub-

(continued)

headings and summary statements usually presented at the end of the material. Just reading the questions at the end of a chapter in a textbook can give you a general idea of the content. This is sometimes called pre-reading or previewing.

Which of the following materials do you think should be read primarily with the purpose of getting a general idea of the content?

an assigned chapter from your textbook	☐	See ⑱
the <u>Playboy</u> centerfold	☐	See ⑲
outside reading assignments	☐	See ⑳

---

⑱   Let's hope you don't! If you are reading an assigned chapter, you are probably trying to get <u>detailed</u> information, not general information, so that you can do well in class discussion or on a test.

Return to ⑰ and try again.

---

⑲   Hmmm. Do you also get pleasure from reading about protein molecules? Most people look at the <u>Playboy</u> centerfold in great detail rather than a quick general look. Oh, well, it takes all kinds. We all have our favorite protein molecules.

Go back to ⑰ and try another answer.

---

⑳   That's right. It is generally impossible to read all assignments closely. Your best bet is to read supplemental or outside reading assignments more generally than you do your textbook assignments. The textbook should always be read more carefully than outside readings unless your teacher says otherwise.

Go on to ㉑ .

㉑   Purpose #4: <u>Reading to Locate Specific Information</u>

When you know what you are looking for, you can skim and skip over material at very rapid rates. For instance, if your purpose is to find the definition of a word in the dictionary, or locate what time and channel "Gunsmoke" will be on TV, or who invented the first compass, or how many eggs you will need to follow the recipe you want to use, you are reading for the purpose of <u>locating specific information</u>.

Which of the following situations would include reading primarily for the purpose of locating specific information?

relaxing with the evening newspaper   ☐   See ㉒

reviewing for a test   ☐   See ㉓

㉒   No. Remember, when you read for the purpose of locating specific information, you know ahead of time what you are looking for. If you can just relax with the newspaper, you will probably be looking for something interesting to read about.

     Go to ㉓ .

㉓   Right. Reviewing for a test is a good example of reading to locate specific information. You will be reading to find answers to questions in the text, or questions in a study guide the instructor has given you. Other examples of reading for specific information are locating items on maps, tables, graphs, and charts, finding things in the yellow pages, locating information in <u>Who's Who</u> or biographical dictionaries, and on and on. In other words, you do not read everything; you zero in on the specific information you need.

     Go to ㉔ .

㉔   Purpose #5: <u>Reading to Critically Evaluate</u>

A good education should help you form your own opinions about things. When you are asked to read materials which disagree with your viewpoints, you should open your mind to what the author says and critically evaluate or judge his ideas against your own. You should ask whether or not the author has more evidence than you, whether his evidence is up to date, and whether it is valid information. You should also look for bias and propaganda on the author's part and on your part, too. The main thing is to read with an open mind. When possible, try to read at least two different viewpoints before you make up your mind about an issue. If your education doesn't help you change your mind about some things you've always accepted as gospel truth, then you've been cheated somewhere along the line.

(continued)

Which of the following materials should be read primarily for the purpose of critically evaluating?

a magazine article claiming sexual intercourse causes cancer

☐ See (25)

directions for installing a dishwasher

☐ See (26)

a textbook chapter on techniques for solving algebraic equations

☐ See (27)

---

(25)   You'd better believe it! An article like that ought to be read very critically.

Go on to (28) .

---

(26)   No. That type of material should be read more for Purpose #2: Reading for Practical Application. Critical evaluation can be applied to everything you read, but it is more appropriately applied to materials which deal in opinions and speculation rather than fact.

Return to (24) and try another answer.

---

(27)   More than likely, no. You'd probably read about techniques for the purpose of gaining information for application—Purpose #2. Critical evaluation should generally be applied to materials which are controversial or opinionated, such as editorials in newspapers and magazines, prepared political statements, historical articles, movie and book reviews, and other materials which deal more in opinion than fact.

Return to (24) and select another answer.

---

(28)   The five purposes which have just been presented to you were not handed down from God. There are certainly other purposes for reading. However, the differences in each purpose mentioned here should show you that before you read anything, you should ask yourself what your purpose for reading is. Sometimes you have to create your own purpose which may not even have been mentioned here. For instance, you don't always watch television with the same purpose. Sometimes you select a program for pleasure, sometimes because of the actors, sometimes because there is nothing better on TV, sometimes because a friend has recommended

it, sometimes because you want certain information, and sometimes because an instructor has assigned it. In other words, your whole approach to watching the program will be based on your purpose for viewing it. How much you get out of the program, how involved you get in it, or how much you remember about it all depends on your purpose. The same thing applies to reading.

Now, here's a little self-check to see how well you have understood this section on purpose in reading. There are two columns below. Fill in the blanks in the first column (types of reading purposes) with the letters in the second column (types of reading materials).

_____ 1. reading for pleasure   a. this reading skills book

_____ 2. reading for practical application   b. the newspaper

    c. a textbook index

_____ 3. reading for general information

    d. an editorial on legalizing marijuana

_____ 4. reading to locate specific information

    e. a mystery novel

_____ 5. reading to critically evaluate

Check your answers in (29) .

---

(29)   Compare your answers with these:

   e   1. reading for pleasure (discussed in (9))

   a   2. reading for practical application (discussed in (13))

   b   3. reading for general information (discussed in (17))

   c   4. reading to locate specific information (discussed in (21))

   d   5. reading to critically evaluate (discussed in (24))

If you missed any of the above, it is strongly recommended that you return to the frame indicated and reread it. When you feel that you understand it, go to (P1) in the Practice Exercises, which begin on page 53.

If you got all the answers correct—fantastic! Go back to (3) .

Remember that you got here by responding to statements at the beginning of this chapter.

(30)   <u>Recognizing</u> <u>and</u> <u>Understanding</u> <u>Main</u> <u>Ideas</u> <u>and</u> <u>Supporting</u> <u>Details</u>

If you checked items 3 or 4 or both on the check list, you belong here.

Otherwise, go back to **(3)**.

This section will deal with learning how to recognize the difference between main ideas and supporting details so that you can remember better what is read. Understanding the organizational pattern an author uses actually aids your memory. You will not only comprehend better, but you will remember longer what you have read.

As you probably know, the topic sentence of a paragraph is the one which states the paragraph's subject. Usually, though not always, the topic sentence is the first one. Sometimes it is a combination of the first and last sentences in the paragraph. Frequently, the main idea is expressed in the topic sentence, but often you the reader must determine what the main idea of a paragraph is by summarizing what is said and putting it all together yourself.

Here is a sample paragraph. Underline what you think is the <u>main</u> <u>idea</u> of the paragraph.

> There are five basic methods for developing a more powerful vocabulary. The first method is to memorize words by sight recognition by making vocabulary cards for words that you want to learn. A second method is to learn phonetics so that you can sound out words you can't recognize by sight but may recognize when you hear them. Another method is to learn words by their use in context as you read. A fourth method is to learn word structure, such as the meanings of roots, prefixes, and suffixes. The last method, and probably the least effective, is to turn to a dictionary for word study.

Do your underlining, then go to **(31)** to check your markings.

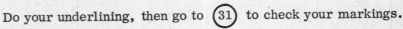

---

(31)   A good way to help separate main ideas from details is to mark the passages as you read. On the next page is how you might have marked the sample paragraph in **(30)**.

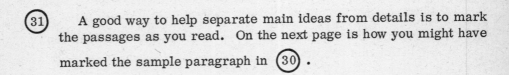

main idea —

There are five basic methods for developing a more powerful vocabulary. The first method is to memorize words by sight recognition by making vocabulary cards for words you want to learn.   A second method is to learn phonetics so that you can sound out words you can't recognize by sight but may recognize when you hear them.   Another method is to learn words by their use in context as you read.   A fourth method is to learn word structure, such as the meanings of roots, prefixes, and suffixes.   The last method, and probably the least effective, is to turn to a dictionary for word study.

supporting details

You should have underlined the first sentence or at least the words five basic methods for developing vocabulary.   Like most (but not all) paragraphs, the topic sentence is stated in the first sentence.   In this case, the topic sentence happens to state the main idea, too.   The sample paragraph states that there are five ways to build a vocabulary.   The rest of the paragraph consists of details related to the main idea.   The details state what the five methods are.   Thus, you have the following:

Main Idea: five methods for building vocabulary

Supporting Details: sight recognition
                     phonetics (sound)
                     context (use)
                     structure (word parts)
                     dictionary

If you have trouble remembering what you read, you might try taking notes as you read, notes similar to those shown above.   As you study, simply stop reading occasionally and jot down the main idea and the supporting details of the passage you are reading.   This physical act alone will help you better remember what you have read.

Both note-taking and marking are helpful methods for forcing you to pay attention to what is being said.   The result is that your mind can't think about other things when you read and you will remember better what you have read.

Now go to (32) for another exercise on this reading skill.

Here is another sample paragraph. Underline, if possible, what you think is the main idea. Then circle the key words that show the supporting details just as the previous example shows.

> (1) Literal comprehension is what you use to understand and recall main ideas, to follow directions, and to follow a sequence of events. (2) Critical comprehension is what you use to distinguish fact from opinion, to recognize bias, propaganda, and an author's inference, and to evaluate. (3) Aesthetic comprehension is the awareness of style, humor, satire, and quality in writing. (4) Thus, there are three levels of comprehension needed for total comprehension.

If you think the main idea is sentence 1, go to .

If you think the main idea is sentence 2, go to .

If you think the main idea is sentence 3, go to .

If you think the main idea is sentence 4, go to .

---

(33)   Sorry, wrong number. The entire paragraph is not about literal comprehension. That's only part of the paragraph's content.

Look again at the paragraph in and select another answer.

---

(34)   'Fraid not. Critical comprehension is only one type of comprehension discussed.

Return to (32) and try another answer.

---

(35)   Nope. Sentence 3 is a supporting detail. Try another answer. Return to (32) .

---

(36)   Good. You must have noticed that the last sentence is the most general statement and mentions that there are "thus" three levels of comprehension. Sentences 1, 2, and 3 are all supporting details.

Go to (37) .

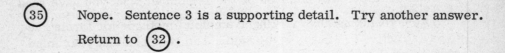

(37)   Now compare your markings on the paragraph sample in (32) with the one below.

supporting details

(1) (Literal comprehension) is what you use to understand and recall main ideas, to follow directions, and to follow a sequence of events. (2) (Critical comprehension) is what you use to distinguish fact from opinion, to recognize bias, propaganda, and an author's inference, and to evaluate. (3) (Aesthetic comprehension) is the awareness of style, humor, satire, and quality in writing. (4) Thus, there are <u>three levels of comprehension needed for</u> <u>total comprehension.</u>   } *main idea*

Go to (38) .

(38)   Pretend now that you did not mark the paragraph but that instead you were taking notes. Fill in the blanks below with the appropriate answers.

Main Idea: _____

Supporting Details: _____

_____

_____

_____

Compare your answer with mine in (40) .

(39)   If you think the main idea of frames (29) to (40) is to show you the difference between main ideas and details, go to (41) now.

No, don't read on; go to (41) now!

If you think the main idea of frames (29) to (40) is to show you how to mark a book or take notes from a book, go to (42) .

(40)   Your outline should look like this:

Main Idea: three levels of comprehension

Supporting Details: (1) literal level
                     (2) critical level
                     (3) aesthetic level

Notice that the main idea is a general statement. Details are more specific.

"But what if I have an instructor who wants to know what is meant by literal, critical, and aesthetic levels of comprehension?" you ask.

That's no big deal. You just have to learn to be even more specific so that maybe your notes read like this:

Main Idea: three levels of comprehension

Supporting Details: (1) literal level

                          a. recognize main ideas
                          b. follow directions
                          c. sequence of events

                     (2) critical level

                          a. fact vs. opinion
                          b. recognize bias, propaganda
                          c. recognize author's inference
                          d. evaluate

                     (3) aesthetic level

                          a. awareness of style, humor, satire
                          b. awareness of quality

"Good grief!" you say. "Do I have to go through all that with everything I read?"

To be perfectly honest, yes and no. If you can separate main ideas from details in your mind without doing all this, the answer is no. If you have never had much experience in doing this type of activity, then yes. Practice doing this with some of your reading assignments until you can do it in your head. In time, you will find you only have to mark or take notes on certain types of materials. But reading about it here won't help one bit unless you try marking or taking notes on textbook material you have to read for your course work.

Try these methods on your next reading assignment.

Go to (39) .

(41)   You're right. It may be that you don't actually need to mark or take notes from your books to recognize details from main ideas. Marking and note-taking are just useful devices to help you see the difference.

Now go back to (3), the check list.

---

(42)   Wrong. The main idea of those frames is to help you see the difference between main ideas and supporting details. The techniques of marking and taking notes from your book are methods for helping you distinguish between main ideas and details, not the main idea of the section. In other words, one of the tasks in reading is to distinguish main ideas from supporting information. The methods of marking and note-taking shown here are merely devices or ways you can learn to achieve the ability to separate details from main points.

Now go to (43) for another reading skill exercise.

---

(43)   To make certain you are on solid ground, read the following paragraph. Mark it if you want, but read with the purpose of distinguishing the main idea from supporting details.

> Skim reading is a valuable skill to develop because of the time it can save you. While it should never be used as a replacement for thorough reading, skimming can be used when your purpose is to read only for the main ideas or general content of a reading selection, or when you know in advance what you are looking for, such as a telephone number in a directory, a word in a dictionary, a catalogue item in the library, or an entry in the index of a book. It is also a timesaving device if used properly to help you look over books placed on reserve in the library by your instructor or to cover books listed on an instructor's supplemental reading list. The wise student realizes he can't read everything recommended by all his instructors. Skimming can at least help you become aware of the general content of many of those recommended books.

Now fill in the blanks on the next page, basing your answers on the paragraph you just read.

(continued)

Main Idea: _____

Supporting Details: _____

_____

_____

_____

_____

Complete the outline, then check your answer in (44) .

---

(44)   The main idea of the sample paragraph is that skimming is a timesaver and a useful skill (note the first sentence). Support of this point consists of the following details. It's a useful skill:

(a) when looking for main ideas.
(b) when you know what you are looking for (such as telephone numbers, words in a dictionary, or catalogue items).
(c) when you have to read reserved library books.
(d) when you have to read supplemental books.

If your answers were quite different from these, you need more practice. Go to (P1) .

If your answers were similar to these, smile at yourself in the nearest mirror and go back to (4) .

---

(45)   Understanding Relationships

You shouldn't be here unless you checked item 5 on the check list at the beginning of the chapter. It's not that there are any secrets here; it's just that you're wasting your time otherwise. This section of frames deals with understanding relationships.

Authors can develop the main ideas of their paragraphs by using a variety of methods. Among the most used are:

Use of examples or illustrations which support or give meaning to the main idea of the paragraph.

Use of comparison or contrast to show similarities or differences which can help clarify the main idea.

Use of definition to give meaning or clarification to the topic being discussed.

Use of explanation or description to expand or clarify the main idea.

Use of a combination of any of the preceding four methods.

The ability to recognize how an author develops his main ideas is called understanding relationships in a paragraph. This means you can see how each sentence in the paragraph relates to the topic sentence and how the topic sentence relates to the main idea of the paragraph.

Read the following paragraph. It is one you may have already read in the practice paragraphs, but we want to show you something you may not have noticed.

> (1) There is an abundance of game in the area. (2) Mammals you are most likely to see include antelope, ground squirrel, cottontail, and jackrabbit. (3) Also present are mule deer, bobcat, coyote, gray fox, skunk, and badger. (4) Common birds are the scaled quail, brown towhee, redtailed hawk, and house finch. (5) Lizards are prevalent, as is the harmless gopher snake. (6) The prairie rattlesnake, the only poisonous reptile in the area, is seldom seen.

The main idea of the paragraph is expressed best in sentence number _____.

Which of the following terms best explains how the author develops his main idea in the paragraph?

☐ 1.   the use of definition to give meaning to the main idea

☐ 2.   the use of examples and illustrations to explain the main idea

☐ 3.   the use of comparison and contrast to show similarities and differences

☐ 4.   the use of explanation to expand the main idea or clarify meaning

Check your responses in ④⑦ .

(46) Vocalization

If you checked item 7, you are in the right place. If you didn't, go away.

The pencil wiggling and falling from your lips is an indication that you move your lips when you read silently. This is a "no-no" in reading called vocalization. Vocalization is fine when you are reading poetry or plays, but for normal reading, it slows you down to at least half the speed you could be reading. Some psychologists suggest that vocalizing as you study helps reinforce what you read. Others disagree.

While vocalization isn't as serious as lung cancer, it can be serious enough to keep you from doing your homework and other reading in much less time. What you are doing is forming the sound of every word you read and probably relying on the sound of the word rather than the sight of the word to give you meaning.

Here's a simple way to lick the vocalization problem. Stick that pencil back between your lips and practice reading for a while. Do all your reading for the next two weeks with a pencil between your lips. When it falls out, put it back in. Soon the problem will disappear. All you really needed was to have your attention called to what you were doing. (And a tasty pencil.)

 Now go back to (7).

---

(47) The main idea of the paragraph is expressed in sentence 1: There is an abundance of game in the area. The author then gives you examples of the type of game in the area. In sentences 2 and 3 he gives you examples of mammals. In sentence 4 he gives examples of birds in the area. Then, in sentences 5 and 6, he gives examples of reptiles. Thus, the author develops his main idea in the paragraph through the use of examples. You should have checked box number 2.

Now move on to (48).

---

(48) Read the following paragraph and answer the questions which follow.

(1) In later centuries, the native Americans known as the Basketmakers adopted many new ideas which were introduced into the Southwest. (2) This included such things

as the making of pottery, the bow and
arrow, bean cultivation, and new styles
in housemaking. (3) They no longer
lived in pit houses, gradually changing
their homes to rectangular houses of
stone masonry above the ground.
(4) These were connected together and
became "apartment house" villages.

1.   Which sentence contains the main idea? _____

2.   Which of the following best explains the relationships or
use of the sentence in the paragraph? _____

    a. examples/illustrations
    b. comparison/contrast
    c. definition
    d. explanation/description
    e. combination

Check your answers in (50) .

---

(49)   Here is another paragraph to read. Look for the type of relationships used in each sentence to support the main idea.

      (1) My first trip underwater was like
slipping into another world. (2) The coral
was so colorful—brown, beige, violet, and
green. (3) It was all shapes and sizes.
(4) Some was round, some flat, some
branched and covered with sea plants that
wave to and fro in the current.

1.   Which sentence contains the main idea? _____

2.   Which pattern of relationships best describes the way the
main idea is developed? _____

    a. example/illustration
    b. comparison/contrast
    c. definition
    d. explanation/description
    e. combination

Check your answers in (52) .

1. The main idea is in sentence 1.

2. The answer to the second question could be a or e. Sentence 2 is definitely a because it gives examples of the changes in the Basketmakers' culture. Sentences 3 and 4, however, give explanations or descriptions of the changes made in one area—housemaking. Thus, e is actually the best answer. Give yourself credit if you marked a, however. You're learning!

Now go back to 49 .

---

(51) Read the following paragraph and once again look for the type of relationship used to support the main idea.

> (1) It's 32 feet long, has velvet drapery, a purple-paneled refrigerator, a miniature bathroom with tub and shower, a built-in color TV, sleeps eight, and cruises U.S. highways at 60 mph. (2) What is it? (3) Why, one of the five million recreational vehicles that are part of the rapidly growing leisure industries of the nation.

1. Which sentence contains the main idea? _____

2. Which pattern of relationships best describes the way the main idea is developed? _____

   a. example/illustration
   b. comparison/contrast
   c. definition
   d. explanation/description
   e. combination

Check your answers in (53) .

---

1. The answer is sentence 1.

2. The answer is d because sentences 2, 3, and 4 all describe what it was like underwater—another world. The paragraph describes by giving colors, shapes, sizes so that we can understand better what the author means by underwater being another world. You may have marked a as the answer, but look again at the paragraph. It does more describing than listing of examples.

Try (51) now.

---

(53) 1. The answer is sentence 3.

2. The best answer is e, although you might have marked either c or d. Sentence 1 gives a description of a recreational vehicle so that you could say c. On the other hand, sentence 2 says, "What is it?" which means sentence 3 is also defining a type of recreational vehicle. Since both methods are used, e is perhaps the best answer. The main thing is to notice the relationships between the sentences and the main idea.

Take a look at (54) now.

---

(54) Here is still another paragraph for you to read in our seemingly never-ending quest for the understanding of relationships in paragraphs.

> (1) In the past, camping used to mean backpacks, tents, canned food, and rubbing two sticks together for fire. (2) Campers expected to do without such things as hot water baths, ice in their drinks, and warm, comfortable beds. (3) Now, however, the modern recreational campers have changed all that. (4) The majority of campers today now have self-contained units providing stoves, refrigerators, hot running water, and modern plumbing.

1. Which sentence contains the main idea? _____

2. Which pattern of relationships best describes the way the main idea is developed? _____

   a. example/illustration
   b. comparison/contrast
   c. definition
   d. explanation/description
   e. combination

Check your answers in (56) .

Caught you snooping! Get back to the frame where you belong.

 1. The main idea is in sentence 3—modern recreational vehicles have changed camping.

2. The best answer is b, comparison/contrast. Sentences 1 and 2 show the way camping used to be. Sentence 4 shows the contrast or differences now with modern camping facilities.

Move on now to .

 This is the last paragraph reading exercise in understanding relationships in paragraphs. Read it and answer the questions which follow.

> (1) There is a reading deficiency called strephosymbolia (pronounced stref-o-sim-bo-le-ah). (2) The name was coined by Orton and refers to the perception of words or letters as if they were reversed by a mirror. (3) In more simple language, strephosymbolia means the twisting of symbols or letters so that words such as <u>saw</u> look like <u>was</u>, or <u>god</u> like <u>dog</u>. (4) In milder form, some readers twist or reverse only certain letters rather than whole words.

1. Which sentence contains the main idea? _____

2. Which pattern of relationships best describes the way the

main idea is developed? _____

   a. example/illustration
   b. comparison/contrast
   c. definition
   d. explanation/description

Check your answers in .

 1. The main idea is not really stated in any one sentence, although sentence 1 could be marked. The main idea of the paragraph is to define strephosymbolia.

2.   c, definition. All the sentences attempt to define the term mentioned in sentence 1. Thus the main idea of the paragraph is the intent to define strephosymbolia.

If you did not do well on these last few exercises on recognizing relationships, go to (P16) for more practice.

If you did well on these, go back to (5). Remember that you got here by answering a check list at the beginning of the chapter.

(59)   Critical <u>Reading</u>

You don't belong here unless you checked item 6 on the check list. If you have trouble reading critically and understanding an author's purpose, you're in the right place.

Reading critically is the process of being aware of an author's intent or the point of his writing, his use of facts, his attitude and bias toward his subject matter, and your own bias toward a subject. To read critically you must be able to:

> Understand what the author is saying and his intent.

> Distinguish fact from opinion; fact is something which is accepted as truth or can be tested and proven, while an opinion is a belief or feeling about something.

> Examine the source, such as knowing who the author is, his reliability, his viewpoints and bias.

> Detect the author's attitude and his use of emotionalism, inferences, and logic.

> Be aware of your own prejudices and how they might keep you from reading critically if you easily accept or reject what you read.

Learning to do all this is not easy. It requires that you begin to question everything you read by automatically doing the above five steps. Critical reading requires that you "talk back" to the author rather than merely accept what you read. That includes what's in this book, too!

Not enough practice on critical reading can possibly be given in this book, but the following exercises should help you on your way if you continue to apply what you have covered so far, plus what you are going to learn. If you are really "gung ho" about learning to

(continued)

read critically, you may wish to read Richard Altick's <u>Preface</u> <u>to</u> <u>Critical</u> <u>Reading</u>. It's probably in your school or local library and reading it would be well worth your time. But we can get you started here and now.

Read critically the following paragraph and look for the author's intent towards his subject and his attitude. This means not only recognizing the main idea but also his reason for writing and how he seems to feel about his subject. Try this exercise and it will become clearer.

(1) In 1855, with the help of Sam Houston, the Coushatta Indians in Texas tried once more to obtain the lands which had been promised to them years before. (2) In consideration for their services to their country and their devotion to the early settlers of Texas, the Coushattas were granted a tract of six hundred and forty acres. (3) Through some political "mixup," the land was never "located" for them. (4) Once again promises to Indians were not kept.

See if you can answer these questions correctly.

1. The author's intent or purpose is to

   ☐ a. make the Coushattas look unfavorable.

   ☐ b. gain Indian support.

   ☐ c. show injustices done to Coushattas.

2. Judging from the way the paragraph is written, the author's attitude towards the Coushatta Indians probably is

   ☐ a. favorable.

   ☐ b. unfavorable.

   ☐ c. unable to tell.

3. Do you agree with the author that "Once again promises to Indians were not kept"? _____ Why? _____

_____

Check your answers in ⑥①.

(60)   Here's another paragraph to read looking for an author's intent, attitude, and bias.

> (1) The new proposition regarding assign-
> ment of students to schools is weak. (2) Its
> first sentence proposes some deceptively
> simple language which has already been de-
> clared unconstitutional by the Supreme Court.
> (3) Secondly, the proposition repeals an ad-
> ministrative process whereby local school
> boards are to plan ahead, within districts
> where problems exist, to solve educational
> inequities. (4) Passage of the proposition will
> only encourage court-ordered "busing."

1.   The author's intent is to

☐   a.   encourage support of the proposition.

☐   b.   discourage support of the proposition.

☐   c.   unable to tell.

2.   The author's attitude towards the proposition is

☐   a.   favorable.

☐   b.   unfavorable.

☐   c.   unable to tell.

3.   Is the writing convincing to you? _____ Why?

Check your answers in (62) .

(61)   1.   c, show injustice. Notice in sentence 1: "tried once more," which implies other attempts; notice, too, all of sentence 3. The author obviously wants to show poor treatment given the Indians.

2.   a, favorable. Although you don't know the author's <u>real</u> feelings, at least the way the paragraph is composed shows he wants the reader to be on the side of the Indian. Sentence 2 praises the Coushattas. Sentences 1 and 3 show the prob-lems they had getting what was rightfully theirs.

3.   Answers will vary because of different readers' bias. Your own bias becomes evident in your answer. You may <u>think</u>

(continued)

you are pro-Coushattas because you have heard of all the different broken treaties with Indians. But is your answer based on fact or emotion? What do you really know about the subject? (As it turns out, the paragraph is based on fact found in the Bureau of Indian Affairs office.)

Now go to .

---

1. b, discourage support. Notice sentence 4.

2. b, unfavorable. Notice the use of the word "weak" in sentence 1, the use of "deceptively" and "unconstitutional" in sentence 2.

3. Answers will vary. Whether or not it is convincing to you depends on your acceptance of the author's statement that the proposition is "unconstitutional" and your own bias toward "busing." (Actually, there is not enough information in this one paragraph to convince a truly critical reader. The "other side of the coin" needs to be heard before a final decision is made. That would be true critical reading.)

Now go to (63) .

---

(63) Read critically the following paragraph looking for the author's intent, attitude, and bias.

(1) What constitutes a critical reader?
(2) First, a critical reader must be biased.
(3) Not prejudiced, which he would be if he has formed conclusions without, or in spite of, supporting evidence; but biased, when he has come to a sincere conclusion on the basis of his background of experience with the subject in question. (4) In other words, he must have a stand on the subject under investigation.
(5) If he has no stand—we use the term "open mind," though "empty mind" would sometimes be more appropriate—he may accept the first presentation which reaches him because he lacks sufficient background to dispute the point. (6) At best, he can delay final acceptance of the information pending direct experience or further consultation with other sources.

1. What is the author's intent?

    ☐ a. to define a critical reader

    ☐ b. to define bias

    ☐ c. unable to tell

2. What is the author's attitude towards his subject?

    ☐ a. serious

    ☐ b. light-hearted

    ☐ c. unable to tell

3. Do you agree or disagree with the author? _____

    Why? _____

Check your answers in ⑥④ .

---

⑥④ 1. a, to define a critical reader. He also defines what he means by bias, but his basic intent is to define by answering his question in sentence 1. (Did you note the use of definition in getting across his main idea? Remember to keep using all the skills you have learned so far.)

2. a, serious.

3. Answers will vary, but in the bias of this author, he does a good job of defining not only a critical reader's reaction to material but also his meaning of the word bias. You would do well to follow the advice given in sentences 5 and 6.

Go to ⑥⑤ now.

---

⑥⑤ Read critically the following paragraph and answer the questions which follow.

(1) According to the Reverend David A. Noebel in his pamphlet "Communism, Hypnotism and the Beatles," the Beatles in particular and rock and roll music in general are all part of the Communists' Master Music Plan to undermine the morals of America's youth. (2) Communist scientists, educators and political leaders are using the Beatles and music

(continued)

like theirs to send our youth into nervous convulsions, confusion, sexual acts and drugs. (3) Noebel writes that the findings of Ivan P. Pavlov, the famous Russian physiologist, regarding conditioned reflexes were used by Lenin in his plans to obtain the Russian people's willing cooperation in changing behavior patterns during the Russian revolution. (4) These findings are now being used through rock music to create hysteria and social rebellion among America's youth. (5) As Noebel says, "Throw away your Beatle and rock and roll records in the city dump. . . let's make sure four mop-headed, anti-Christ beatniks don't destroy our children's emotional and mental stability. . . ."

1. Which of the following best describes the author's intent?

☐ a. to show rock music is communistically inspired

☐ b. to prove how the Beatles are part of the Master Music Plan

☐ c. to tell readers of Noebel's belief in the Communists' Master Music Plan

2. What is the author's attitude?

☐ a. serious

☐ b. emotional

☐ c. sarcastic

3. To the best of your knowledge, which sentences are factual? (Use sentence numbers.) _____

4. Which sentences are opinion? _____

5. Do you agree or disagree with the author? _____

Why? _____

6. Are you biased toward the subject? _____

Check your answers in .

---

  1. c is the best answer because the author does not <u>show</u> rock music is communistically inspired, nor does he <u>prove</u> the Beatles are part of the Master Music Plan. His intent is to

warn the reader or at least make the reader aware of the Communists' use of rock music in their Master Plan. The author apparently believes what Noebel believes because he also advises the reader to throw away rock and roll records. The last sentence in particular shows his concern.

2. a, serious, although he does use an emotional appeal by making it sound as though the Communists are out to destroy "America's youth" and that social rebellion among youth is inspired by rock music.

3. Sentences 1, 3, and 5. All refer to Noebel's pamphlet and thus can be checked on for accuracy. Note: They may be factually reported from Noebel's pamphlet, but that does not mean what Noebel says is factual.

4. Sentences 2 and 4 sound factual but there is no proof of this in the paragraph (or anywhere else this author knows). They are opinions until proven with facts.

5. Answers will vary, but personally (and you do not have to agree), I can't buy the claim because there are not enough facts to back up what the author says. I would like some proof that there even is a Master Music Plan, that "Communist scientists and educators" are using rock music to bring about hysteria, or that "four mop-headed, anti-Christ beatniks" (a rather poor and emotionally charged description of the Beatles) are destroying our children's emotional stability. But then, I'm prejudiced because I like the Beatles' music. Perhaps my moral stability has been destroyed already!

6. Answers will vary. As I said, I am biased against the intent, attitude, and subject matter. I'm also biased against the author because he uses a minister's writings as his source and I don't believe Reverend Noebel is an authority on the subject. But you don't have to agree. In fact, it's healthy to disagree with me and any other writer you read. Just because something is in print, doesn't mean it is true. That goes for what I say as well as Reverend Noebel.

Try another critical reading exercise in .

  Read critically the paragraph which begins on the next page. It is from an article entitled "Capital Punishment: Your Protection and Mine." The author is Edward J. Allen, Chief of Police in Santa Ana, California when he wrote this.

(continued)

(1) Parole and probation people, an occasional governor, prison wardens (some prefer to be called penologists), criminal lawyers, and oftentime prison chaplains advance this "no deterrent" point of view [the idea that capital punishment does not deter crime]. (2) None doubts their sincerity, but they are hardly in a qualified position to speak on the matter authoritatively or with pure objectivity. (3) How can they possibly know how many people are not on death row because of the deterrent effect of the death penalty? (4) Neither do they see the vicious, often sadistic despoiler or the cold-blooded professional killer plying their murderous trades. (5) They encounter these predatory creatures after their fangs have been pulled; after they have been rendered harmless, deprived of the weapons and the opportunities to commit additional crimes. (6) Naturally, in their cages they behave more like sheep than ravenous wolves.

1. Which of the following best describes the author's intent in the paragraph?

☐   a. to show that people who advocate the death penalty be abolished don't know what they are talking about

☐   b. to show that murderers are vicious and should receive the death penalty

☐   c. to show that parole and probation people, criminal defense attorneys, and penologists are not sincere

2. Which of the following best describes the author's attitude toward his subject?

☐   a. serious

☐   b. sarcastic

☐   c. unable to tell

3. Which sentences are factual statements? (List by number.)

_____

4. Which sentences are statements of opinion? _____

5. Do you agree or disagree with the author? _____

Why? _____

6.   Are you biased toward the subject? _____

Check your responses in (68) .

---

(68) 1.   a. Notice that sentence 2 does not doubt their sincerity and
            sentence 3 raises the author's intent. He tries to answer
            his own question in the remainder of the paragraph.

      2.   a, serious. You might even say "dead serious." (Bad
            joke?) Notice the serious tone given through the use of
            words and phrases such as "vicious," "sadistic," "cold-
            blooded professional killer," and "ravenous wolves." All
            are used to describe the type of person the author feels de-
            serves the death penalty. He is loading his paragraph with
            words he hopes will convince you of his stand.

      3.   Sentence 1 is rather factual. If you have read much about
            the death penalty or if you have heard people argue against
            it, you know that many of them fit into the categories he
            lists. It is easy enough to check through research. It's
            about the only sentence in the paragraph I feel comes close
            to being factual and wouldn't argue too strongly against you
            if you disagreed.

      4.   Most of the sentences are opinions. This does not mean his
            points might not be proven factual, but the author uses some
            loaded words, some mentioned before, plus these: "plying
            their murderous trades," "predatory creatures," "fangs,"
            and "cages"—all of which give an animal image to those per-
            sons he feels deserve the death penalty. My question is,
            "Do all persons given the death penalty fit these terms?"
            Perhaps, but frankly, I don't know.

      5.   Answers will vary. Make certain your answer is not an
            emotionally based one. For my part, I've done quite a lot
            of reading on the subject and I still don't know how I feel
            about it. I lean towards its abolishment, but sometimes I
            waver. What about you?

      6.   Answers will vary. I'm not biased myself; more like con-
            fused. It's a subject I need to think more about.

Hopefully, some of the questions and answers given in this section
have shown you that there are no right or wrong answers to some
critical questions. The intent has been to show you that some books
and articles are not well written or factually correct. As a critical
reader, don't be afraid to disagree with an author or the answers
to his questions!

(continued)

If you did well on these last exercises, go to (6).

If you want more practice on critical reading, go to (P22) now.

(69)   <u>Vocabulary</u> <u>Section</u>

You don't belong here unless you checked item 8 on the check list at the beginning of this chapter. However, you can stay if you're interested in vocabulary improvement.

No one probably need tell you that vocabulary and comprehension are closely related. If you don't understand key words an author uses you may not only miss what he is saying, but also his attitude toward his subject. He could be putting you on and you would never know it!

As you work through this book you will get more drill in vocabulary development. You need, however, a way to remember the words you will be learning. The best method for learning and remembering the words you don't know in this book (or any other words you need to learn) is to use what is known as the vocabulary card technique.

The object of learning new words is to remember them so that you can use them in speaking and writing and to understand their meaning when you read or hear them. There are certain words which you use regularly but never think about—you just use them. When you speak with a friend, you don't analyze every word you are going to say. You have ideas, and certain familiar, "overlearned" words come tumbling out without thinking about them. Overlearning new words means that you can begin to use and recognize them without really thinking about them.

One of the best techniques for overlearning new words is to select one word you feel is important to learn. Print that word on the front of a 3 x 5 card. Notice the example on the next page.

On the back of the card, write the information shown in the lower example on the next page after looking up the word in the dictionary.

ubiquitous

(front of card)

pronounced: yōō-bik'-wə́-təs
definition: seeming to be everywhere
synonyms: everywhere, omnipresent
context: Think of July Fourth,
flags and ball games
and the ubiquitous
frankfurt-and-roll
enters your mental image

(back of card)

If you do this every day, you will begin to have a growing stack
of personal vocabulary cards. The trick is to spend about five or
ten minutes every day going over and over and over the cards.
Remember, you want to "overlearn" them so that you begin using
the words without thinking, just as you use words now without thinking. Carry the cards around in your pocket or bag, or keep them
somewhere you are sure to remember to practice them.

When you have compiled and learned about twenty-five or thirty
cards, get someone to check you by letting them flash the front of

(continued)

the card at you and you pronounce it, give the definition, and then use it in a sentence. The best bet is to have one of your teachers check you so that you know you are pronouncing and using each word correctly.

There are boxes of vocabulary cards already printed and ready for you to learn which can be bought. However, the disadvantage is that the words used are selected by someone else and may not be the words you need to learn.

If you think this method will work for you, get started on it. Then go to (72) .

If you want to read about some other methods for improving your vocabulary, go to (70) .

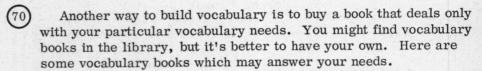

(70)   Another way to build vocabulary is to buy a book that deals only with your particular vocabulary needs. You might find vocabulary books in the library, but it's better to have your own. Here are some vocabulary books which may answer your needs.

Brown, James I. Programmed Vocabulary. Appleton-Century-
  Crofts, 1964.

  This book is programmed for self-study and claims that the mastery of 14 Master Words, their roots and affixes, will help you learn over 14,000 words. While you can use this book on your own, it is not an easy one to work in.

Gilbert, Doris Wilcox. Breaking the Word Barrier. Prentice-
  Hall, 1972.

  This book provides self-inventories of your vocabulary in specific areas such as vocation and industry, health services, business, insurance, and government. It offers a wide variety of drills in prefix, suffix, context, analogies, and word parts.

Feinstein, George W. Programmed College Vocabulary 3600.
  Prentice-Hall, 1969.

  This book is also programmed for self-study. It focuses on literary and academic terms, dealing with Latin and Greek derivatives, descriptive and action words, and technical vocabulary. It is best used in a classroom situation.

Funk, Wilfred and Norman Lewis. 30 Days to a More Powerful Vocabulary. Washington Square Press, 1949.

This book has been around for a long time, and it is a good one. It is not programmed, but it is designed for people who want to spend about 15 minutes a day for 30 days on vocabulary building. This book, along with vocabulary card usage, could prove very helpful if you follow through each day.

Joffee, Irwin L. Developing Vocabulary Skills. Wadsworth Publishing Company, 1971.

A brief book, but provides enough basis for establishing a good vocabulary if you practice with the methods provided.

Taylor, Sanford, et al. Word Clues, Books J, K, L, M. Educational Development Laboratories, 1963.

These are four of several books in a series, each one of different difficulty beginning with the lowest letter. Each book contains 300 words to learn. They are programmed for self-help and provide drills in practically all forms of vocabulary development. Students seem to like working in these books.

There are plenty of vocabulary books around, but these are all texts you can use by yourself and do not require teacher's manuals or answer keys.

If you think this method is best for developing your vocabulary, get an order in for one of the books at your bookstore. You might want to check your library and see if it has any of these books. You could look them over and then decide on the one you want to buy.

When you've done this, go to (72) .

If you want to read about some other methods for improving your vocabulary, go to (71) .

---

(71) Still another way to expand your vocabulary is to learn some basic Greek and Latin word roots and affixes. (Affixes refers to both prefixes and suffixes, or beginnings and endings of words which have special meanings.) The advantage to knowing some Greek and Latin root words is that it can save you many trips to the dictionary when you come across a word that you have never seen before. For instance, what if you reading and were confronted with the word "anthropophobiac"? If you had never seen it before and knew that

(continued)

"anthrop" refers to mankind, "phobia" refers to fear, and that words with "ic" on the end usually mean a person or thing, you could figure out that anthropophobiac means a person who is afraid of man.

You already know many words with Greek and Latin roots. Here are a few.

photograph	photo = light; graph = record of
phonograph	phono = sound; graph = record of
biography	bio = life; graph = record of
telegraph	tele = distance; graph = record or writing
geography	geo = earth; graph = record of

You probably know many more. The point is that this knowledge can be put to use in helping you expand your vocabulary. Following are two lists of words, one Greek roots and the other Latin roots. You may even want to make vocabulary cards for the ones you don't know.

Greek Word Roots and Affixes

Root or Affix	Meaning	Example
amphi	around, both sides	amphitheatre
anti	against	antiaircraft
auto	self	automatic
biblio	book	bibliography
bio	life	biography
dia	across, through	diameter
geo	earth	geography
graph	write, record	graphite
hetero	different, varied	heterogeneous
homo	same, equally mixed	homogenize
macro	large	macroscopic
mania	craze for	pyromania
meter	measure	speedometer
micro	small	microscopic
mono	one	monopoly
peri	around	periscope
philo	love	philosophy
phobos	fear	phobia
phono	sound	phonograph
poly	many	polygamy
scope	examine	periscope
syn	together, with	synchronize
tele	far, distance	telegraph

Latin Word Roots and Affixes

Root or Affix	Meaning	Example
ante	before	antecedent
aqua	water	aqualung
audio	hear	audio
bene	well	benefit
circum	around	circumference
corpus	body	corpse
digit	finger, toe	digital
dorm	sleep	dormitory
duc	lead, take	conductor
ex	out	exit
frater	brother	fraternity
inter	between	interstate
locus	place	locality
mit	send	transmitter
ocul	eye	oculist
pater	father	paternal
ped	foot	pedestrian
port	carry	porter
post	after	postwar
pre	before	predetermine
pro	before	project
scribe	write	transcribe
trans	across	transcontinental
video	see	video

If you are going to use this approach for developing your vocabulary, get started on it now.* Then go to to (72).

If you don't like any of the methods discussed so far, then you're on your own. Maybe you'd better look the three approaches over again and make a decision. Then go to (72).

* For a more indepth look at this approach, you might want to read Jack S. Romine's VOCABULARY FOR ADULTS, another Wiley Self-Teaching Guide.

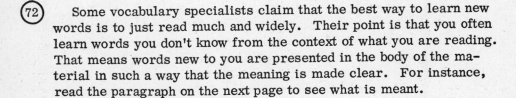

(72) Some vocabulary specialists claim that the best way to learn new words is to just read much and widely. Their point is that you often learn words you don't know from the context of what you are reading. That means words new to you are presented in the body of the material in such a way that the meaning is made clear. For instance, read the paragraph on the next page to see what is meant.

(continued)

The Giants were playing at New York's
Polo Grounds on a chilly day, and the ice
cream and soda pop weren't selling well.
The gloomy concessionaire suddenly remembered the popularity of the hot frankfurt and
roll at the recent World's Fair and decided
to sell it as a cold weather food from then on.
He equipped his vendors with portable hot
water tanks to keep his sausages and rolls hot.
Thus, the "hot dog" spread to baseball.

1. What does the word concessionaire mean here? _____

_____

2. How can you tell, particularly if you've never seen the word

before? _____

The way the word is used here (context) makes it rather easy
for you to figure out the word's meaning if you don't know it. Notice
that the author mentions that ice cream and soda pop weren't selling well. This made the concessionaire gloomy until he remembered
about hot dogs. A concessionaire, then, must be someone who sells
something, in this case, ice cream, soda pop, and hot dogs. A concessionaire, actually, is the person or business granted the privilege of conducting business on premises that don't belong to him.
While all this is not explained in context, at least the way the word
is used in the paragraph offers you a good clue to its general meaning.

Use these clues in all your reading. It's another way to develop
your vocabulary and a necessary part of total comprehension of
what you read.

Now go to ⑦③ .

---

⑦③   Here are some short passages containing words you may or may
not know. Using context clues such as those explained in the preceding frame, write down in the blank spaces what you think are
the meanings of the underlined words in each statement.

1. Abolish all tests and grades. This would destroy the professor's chief weapons of <u>coercion</u>, and would eliminate
two obstacles to the student's learning.

---

2. The first American <u>vendors</u> weren't quite sure how to handle and serve hot dogs.

3. Following the sales slump in 1967 and 1968 created in part by <u>mandatory</u> helmet-use laws. . . , the motorcycle business bounced back.

4. For the <u>novice</u>, I'll quickly try to explain the process so that you can understand what I mean.

5. With all the traffic busily traveling back and forth, I looked for a more <u>secluded</u> road.

Check your answers in .

 1. Since tests and grades are referred to as "weapons" the teacher has against the student, you can guess that coercion must have something to do with force or power over the students. The word refers to forcing someone to do something by force or superior power.

2. The contextual clues are in the words "handle" and "serve." A vendor is someone who sells or peddles something; in this case, hot dogs.

3. Since there were sales slumps because of the helmet-use laws, it can be guessed that mandatory means "must" or to be forced to do something. People didn't buy motorcycles for a while because the law forced them to wear helmets.

4. Since he is going to try to explain a process, a novice must be someone who is not familiar with the process. Actually, a novice is a beginner or someone not familiar with something.

5. The clues here are "traffic" and "busily traveling back and forth." He was looking for a less traffic-congested road, which would be a secluded one—one not traveled by many people. Secluded means hidden away or not easy to find.

These few exercises show you how to find meanings of words in context. We will not give more vocabulary exercises here, but be sure you do this type of activity in your own reading.

(continued)

A vital part of comprehension relies on your word knowledge. Make certain you set up a program for yourself immediately, a program that is easy for you, makes sense for you, and will be carried out by you.

Now go to .

 <u>Timed</u> <u>Reading</u> <u>Selection</u>

This frame and the next will take about fifteen or twenty minutes. If you do not have that much time, do not go on. Come back here when you do.

If you do have time, do not begin until you have access to a watch or a clock with a second hand.

You are going to time yourself while you read from the following selection, "Comprehension Skills." It gives you a chance to read someone else's ideas about comprehension and understanding relationships. You may want to compare and evaluate what you have learned so far with what the article says about comprehension. Judging from the title, state what you think will be your purpose for reading the article.

Your reading purpose: _____

Before you start, think over what you have learned so far about recognizing main ideas, supporting details, understanding relationships, and reading critically. Put it all together and use what you have learned while reading this selection.

Check your watch or clock and write down your starting time when you begin reading. Start exactly on the minute in order to easily determine how many words per minute you will read.

Starting time: _____

Begin reading.

COMPREHENSION SKILLS

by Olive Niles

. . . (1) In the writer's opinion, there are three abilities which clearly differentiate between the reader who comprehends well and the one who does not.

(2) The first of these abilities is the power to find and understand thought relationships: in single sentences, in paragraphs, and in selections of varying lengths. Ideas are related to each other in many ways. Here is a simple example of the most common kind of thought relationship:

> During our visit to the museum, we saw the first Stars and Stripes ever carried in battle; after that we enjoyed a collection of old silverware, later wandered into the room filled with Indian relics, and finally found ourselves absorbed in a display of old wedding gowns.

The parts of this sentence, obviously, are related to each other chronologically. We follow the trip through the museum in the time order in which the rooms were visited.

(3) Now examine the same sentence parts arranged in a different way:

> During our visit to the museum, we saw a collection of old silverware, an absorbing display of old-fashioned wedding gowns, a room filled with Indian relics, and the first Stars and Stripes ever carried in battle.

This sentence tells less than the preceding one. We know what the visitor saw, but we cannot follow him from room to room. The relationship present among the parts of this second sentence is a simple listing.

(continued)

(4) Here is another sentence:

During our visit to the museum, we enjoyed
seeing the first Stars and Stripes ever carried in battle and the absorbing display of
old-fashioned wedding gowns much more
than we did the room filled with Indian relics
and the collection of old silverware.

Now the ideas have a comparison-contrast relationship. The things the author saw have
fallen into two groups: two displays which he
enjoyed, two others he liked much less. An
important additional meaning has been added
because the relationship of the parts of the
sentence is different.

(5) Once more, observe the same facts but
in a fourth relationship:

Because, on our visit to the museum, we
had seen the first Stars and Stripes ever
carried in battle, a room full of Indian
relics, a display of old silverware, and
a collection of old-fashioned wedding gowns,
we were able to present a successful class
program in which we compared relics of
the past with their modern equivalents.

In this last sentence, we have a cause-effect
relationship. The experiences of the museum
visit have produced an effect: a successful
class program.

(6) These four kinds of thought relationship
—time, simple listing, comparison-contrast,
and cause-effect, plus others—occur in a great
many combinations, some of them complex.
The ability to observe and to use these relationships seems to be one of the basic comprehension skills.

(7) The ability to set specific purposes in
reading is a second important ability or skill.
William G. Perry has reported a study done
with fifteen hundred Harvard and Radcliffe
freshmen to determine their habits of study
when presented with a typical chapter in a

history text.* In presenting his results,
Perry has this to say:

> We asked anyone who could do so to
> write a short statement about what the
> chapter was all about. The number
> who were able to tell us . . . was just
> one in a hundred-fifteen. As a demon-
> stration of obedient purposelessness in
> the reading of 99% of freshmen we
> found this impressive . . . after twelve
> years of reading homework assignments
> in school they had all settled into the
> habit of leaving the point of it all to
> someone else.

These same freshmen were able to do very
well on a multiple-choice test based on the
details of the material they had read.

(8) If this purposelessness in study exists
among students like those at Harvard, what
must be the case with others less able? It
might be argued that the moral of the tale is
that teachers should give better assignments
in which they tell students what to look for.
But it would seem more important to suggest
that by the time young people are freshmen at
Harvard, it is high time they know how to set
their own purposes. It is obvious that Perry
questions whether the students he tested had
any real comprehension at all. They could
answer multiple-choice questions, but they
failed to get, as he says, the "point of it all."

(9) Suppose, for example, that a student
is studying a chapter about life on the Southern
plantations. The inefficient reader plods straight
through the material, often with wandering attention because his goal is only to "read the lesson."
Contrast the careful attention to detail, the search
for visual imagery of the student who studies the
same chapter in order to make a drawing of the

(continued)

* William G. Perry, Jr., "Students' Use and Misuse of Reading Skills:
A Report to the Faculty," Harvard Educational Review, Vol. 29, No. 3,
Summer, 1959.

plantation grounds. Contrast again the procedures of the student who wants to compare the way of life of the Southern plantation with that in colonial New England. Or, again, the method used by a student whose responsibility is to report on one very specific topic: the duties of the mistress of the plantation. This last student, if he is reading efficiently, will skim rapidly through the chapter until he comes to a paragraph which seems to have a bearing on his special topic, then settle down to read carefully for detail. The student who thus reads with purpose, and its corollary flexibility, has comprehension impossible to the student who merely "reads."

(10) A third basic comprehension skill is the ability to make full use of previous learning in attacking new material. It is "reading readiness" in an extended form.

(11) Jokes sometimes make an adult realize how a child must feel when he has to read something for which he does not have the requisite readiness. The following is supposed to be a story told by Helen Taft Manning about her father. When Taft was recuperating from a spell of illness, he wired a friend of his recovery and remarked that he had just taken a long horseback ride. The friend wired in reply, "How is the horse?"

(12) Whether the reader sees anything funny at all in this story depends entirely upon whether he happens to remember from his previous reading or from pictures he may have seen that Taft was one of the heftiest of our presidents.

(13) It is partly a matter of chance whether a reader happens to have a fact like this stored up in his head, but there is more to it than chance. Many students actually have the background information for full comprehension but fail to realize that they have it and to use it. Associational reading—the act of drawing upon all one has experienced and read to enrich what he is currently reading—is a skill which can be taught.

(14) To summarize to this point: If an
analysis is made of what lies at the foundation
of comprehension, there seem to be at least
three basic skills, (1) the ability to observe
and use the varied relationships of ideas,
(2) the ability to read with adjustment to conscious purpose, and (3) the ability to make full
use of the backlog of real and vicarious experience which almost every reader possesses.

Record your finishing time. _____ Go to (76) .

(76) Now subtract your starting time from your finishing time to see
how many minutes and seconds it took you to read the article. Use
the space below.

Finishing time.   _____

Starting time.   _____

Total reading time. _____

Use the chart below to figure out how many words per minute
you read. For instance, if you read the article in 4 minutes and
15 seconds, your rate would be 270 words per minute (WPM).

Time	WPM	Time	WPM
1:00	1150	4:00	287
1:15	920	4:15	270
1:30	766	4:30	255
1:45	657	4:45	242
2:00	575	5:00	230
2:15	511	5:15	219
2:30	460	5:30	209
2:45	418	5:45	200
3:00	383	6:00	191
3:15	353	6:15	184
3:30	328	6:30	175
3:45	306	6:45	170

Record your WPM. _____

Go to (77) .

Check your reading comprehension of the selection you just read by answering the following questions. If an answer is false, state why in the blanks.

T / F 1. The author believes that there are four abilities which clearly differentiate between the reader who comprehends well and the one who does not.

_____

T / F 2. The intent of the author in using sample paragraphs about a trip to the museum is to provide examples of what is meant by understanding thought relationships.

_____

T / F 3. In a test of Harvard and Radcliffe freshmen's ability to read a typical chapter in history, it was discovered that while most could write a short statement about what they read, only 1 in 115 did well on a multiple choice test.

_____

T / F 4. It can be inferred from the article that a lack of purpose in reading exists among the best students.

_____

T / F 5. It can be inferred from the article that the author believes Harvard students are among the better students.

_____

T / F 6. One of the basic reading comprehension skills discussed is the ability to observe the relationship of ideas in sentences, paragraphs, and entire written works.

_____

T / F 7. Another basic reading comprehension skill discussed is the ability to read with a purpose.

_____

T / F 8. The ability to use real experiences and knowledge already possessed when reading is necessary to good comprehension.

_____

9. What is the author's purpose in relating the joke about Taft horseback riding?

_____

_____

10. After reading this article, what did you learn about or what do you recall concerning comprehension skills that is similar to or different from what this book has discussed so far?

_____

_____

_____

Now go to (78) .

 Compare your answers with these.

1. False; there are three not four points discussed. This might seem a "nit-picking" question but notice paragraphs 1 and 14 where the purpose and summary are stated. Each time, three points are mentioned. In addition, the entire article is built around these three points.

2. True; see paragraphs 2, 3, 4, 5.

3. False; it was just the opposite. See paragraph 7.

4. True; see paragraph 8.

5. True; again see paragraph 8. The author says, "If this purposelessness . . . exists among students like those at Harvard, what must be the case with <u>others</u> <u>less</u> <u>able</u>?"

6. True; see paragraph 2.

7. True; see paragraphs 7 and 8.

8. True; see paragraphs 10 and 11.

9. To show how previous reading or experience enters into good comprehension. For instance, if you had read this article before today, how much of what you read before would come back to you when you read it again?

10. Answers will vary, of course. It is hoped you learned something. If not, you're either brilliant or need to read it again to find the answer.

(continued)

Go to (79) .

(79)   Count 10 points for each correct answer.

Enter your Comprehension Score here. _____ (In

100 possible points, your score represents a percentage.)

Enter your WPM (words per minute) here. _____

Of nearly 250 freshman city college students in Southern California who took this reading test, the average WPM was 210 words per minute with 70 percent comprehension of the test items. However, reading rates vary with people's interest in the subject, the difficulty of the material being read, and vocabulary and subject matter background. More timed reading selections and comprehension drills are in the third chapter of this book. Use them to help build your reading rate of comprehension, if you need to do so.

This concludes the section on comprehension, but remember, use what you have learned about establishing purpose, recognizing main ideas and supporting details, understanding relationships, and reading critically in all your reading.

If you have not done so, you may wish to work through the following practice exercises on the material in Chapter 1. Otherwise, go on to Chapter 2.

PRACTICE EXERCISES

 OK, here's a chance to show your stuff. Without referring back to the frames you've completed, check your talent by answering the following questions.

1. You were taught that you need to establish a purpose that helps you get involved in your reading. List the purposes discussed in this chapter.

   a. _____

   b. _____

   c. _____

   d. _____

   e. _____

2. Give an example of 1a. _____

3. Give an example of 1b. _____

4. Give an example of 1c. _____

5. Give an example of 1d. _____

6. Give an example of 1e. _____

Check your answers in P3 .

P2 Practices in Recognizing Main Ideas
and Supporting Details

Practice A

Underline what you think is the main idea of the following paragraph and mark the key words and phrases that support the main idea.

> Improving your reading ability is not easy.
> There are no quick-acting pills to take, no
> magic wand to wave over your head. The only
> formula for better reading is steady, conscientious practice. For instance, you should set
> aside a certain portion of each day to practice.
> Don't practice if you are tired—you need a clear
> and alert mind because reading involves thinking.
> Read from a variety of materials and apply different purposes to reading materials so that you
> develop a versatile reading rate.

(continued)

Compare your markings with .

 Your ordering may vary. That's fine. Just make sure your examples fit the right purpose.

1. a. reading for pleasure
    b. reading for practical application
    c. reading for general information
    d. reading to locate specific information
    e. reading to critically evaluate

The following answers will vary but should be similar.

2. reading a mystery novel

3. cookbook, this book, a "how-to" book

4. newspaper, magazine

5. telephone book, dictionary, this answer frame

6. editorials, history textbooks, anything based on someone's opinion

If you came here from frame (29) , go back to frame (3) . If you've finished reading the chapter, go to (P2) .

 The first sentence should be underlined. The key idea is that improving your reading is not easy. Key words and phrases which support this idea are:

"no quick-acting pills"
"no magic wand"
"steady, conscientious practice"
"need a clear and alert mind"
"read from a variety of materials"
"apply different purposes"

Go on to (P5) .

 Practice <u>B</u>

Underline what you think is the main idea of the following paragraph and mark the key words and phrases that support the main idea.

A good reader tries to read more than one side of an issue and is willing to admit that his present opinions on certain subjects may be too narrow or may be wrong. The reason for reading is to broaden one's knowledge. If a reader is only going to read what he already agrees with and close his mind to opposition, he is destroying the purpose and need for education. It is very easy to read and accept those writings with which we already agree. But it is very difficult for us to read objectively writings which contain opinions we disagree with. A good reader, then, tries to read objectively from many sources.

Compare your markings with (P7).

(P6) Using the paragraph in (P5), fill in the blanks below in your own words.

Main Idea: _____

Supporting Details: _____

_____

_____

_____

Check your answers in (P8).

(P7) The last sentence is the key idea or topic sentence. The key words and phrases that support the topic sentence are:

"reads more than one side"
"willing to admit opinions . . . narrow . . . wrong"
"reason for reading . . . broaden . . . knowledge"
"close . . . mind . . . destroying . . . purpose and need for education"
"difficult . . . to read objectively"

Now go back to (P6).

P8   Compare your answers in **P6** with these (wording may vary).

Main Idea: a good reader reads objectively

Supporting Details: reads more than one side
admits it when wrong
reads to broaden knowledge
keeps an open mind

Now go to **P10** .

P9   You don't belong here, but as long as you are, take a rest for a few minutes. Then find your way back to the right frame.

P10   Practice C

Read the paragraph below. Then fill in the blanks which follow.

> There is an abundance of game in the area. Mammals you are most likely to see include antelope, ground squirrel, cottontail, and jackrabbit. Also present are mule deer, bobcat, coyote, gray fox, skunk, and badger. Common birds are the scaled quail, brown towhee, redtailed hawk, and house finch. Lizards are prevalent, as is the harmless gopher snake. The prairie rattlesnake, the only poisonous reptile in the area, is seldom seen.

Main idea: _____

Supporting details: _____

_____

_____

Check your answer in **P12** .

P11   Practice D

Read the paragraph on the next page. Then fill in the blanks which follow.

Thousands of people each year buy books dealing with vocabulary building but never finish them. They start out with good intentions, but too many things "come up" that interfere with completion. Their chances of gaining a better vocabulary are better if they would enroll in a reading or vocabulary class. That way, a portion of time is set aside for self-improvement. Of course, people drop from classes, too. But a heavier commitment to improvement is made through enrollment in a class, more so than merely buying a book and planning to do the work "when there is time."

Main idea: _____

Supporting details: _____

_____

_____

Check your answer in (P13) .

(P12) You probably noticed that the paragraph was about the abundance of game, as stated in the first sentence. The other sentences deal with the type of game, basically mammals, birds, and reptiles. Your answer should read:

Main idea: the abundance of game in the area

Supporting details: mammals (antelope, squirrel, bobcat, etc.)
                     birds (quail, hawk, etc.)
                     reptiles (lizard, gopher snake, rattlesnake)

Go back to (P11) for practice paragraph D.

(P13) Practice paragraph D is a bit more difficult. It is not particularly well-written and while the main idea is stated it is not as clearly stated as in the preceding practice paragraph. Your answer should read:

Main idea: Enrollment in a reading or vocabulary class is a better way to develop a vocabulary than doing it from a book.

(continued)

Supporting details: Most people don't complete the self-help
books they buy.
Too many things "come up" to interfere with
completion of the book.
Enrollment in class is more of a commitment.

Go to   (P14)   for practice paragraph E.

 (P14)   Practice E

Read the following paragraph.   Then fill in the blanks that follow.

In later centuries, the native Americans
known as the Basketmakers adopted many new
ideas which were introduced into the Southwest.   This included such things as the making
of pottery, the bow and arrow, bean cultivation
and new styles in housemaking.   They no longer
lived in pit houses, gradually changing their
homes to rectangular houses of stone masonry
above the ground.   These were connected together and became "apartment house" villages.

Main idea: _____

Supporting details: _____

_____

_____

Check your answers in   (P15) .

 (P15)   The paragraph in Practice E is typical of those paragraphs with
the main idea presented in the first sentence.   Your answers should
read:

Main idea: Basketmakers adopted new ideas in later centuries.

Supporting details: began making pottery
used bow and arrow
new style housemaking—"apartment" villages

By now you should be able to recognize the main ideas in paragraphs.   If you are still having trouble, don't despair.   More exercises appear in the following sections.   You need a change now.

Go back to ⑤ if you came here from frame ㊹ . Otherwise, go to .

 Practices in Understanding Relationships

Practice A

Read the paragraph below. Then answer the questions which follow.

> (1) The new proposition regarding assign-
> ment of students to schools is weak. (2) Its
> first sentence proposes some deceptively
> simple language which has already been de-
> clared unconstitutional by the Supreme Court.
> (3) Secondly, the proposition repeals an ad-
> ministrative process whereby local school
> boards are to plan ahead, within districts
> where problems exist, to solve educational
> inequities. (4) Passage of the proposition
> will only encourage court-ordered "busing."

1. Which sentence in the paragraph best states the main idea?

    (Use sentence number.) _____

2. Which of the following best reflects the pattern of relation-

    ship to the main idea? _____

    a. examples/illustration
    b. comparison/contrast
    c. definition
    d. explanation/description
    e. combination of a, b, c, or d

Check your answers in Ⓟ18 .

 Practice B

Read the paragraph which follows. Then answer the questions.

> (1) There are basically two types of vaca-
> tioners. (2) One is compulsive in his deter-
> mination to throw himself into a whirl of
> activity. (3) Sometimes his vacations turn
> into nightmares of physical exertion and mental

(continued)

exhaustion and he's a wreck by the time he
gets back to work. (4) Then there is the
sedentary type whose thing is slowing down
to a snail's pace.

1. Which sentence in the paragraph best states the main idea?

_____

2. Which of the following best reflects the pattern of relation-

ship to the main idea?

   a. examples/illustration
   b. comparison/contrast
   c. definition
   d. explanation/description
   e. combination

Check your answers in (P19) .

 (P18)

1. The main idea is in sentence 1.

2. Probably d, explanation, is the best choice, although a case
   might be made for a. Sentences 2, 3, and 4 all are examples
   of why the proposition is weak. But here these sentences
   also explain why the author feels the proposition is weak.
   Either answer is acceptable.

Now try (P17) .

 (P19)

1. The main idea is in sentence 1. (Yes, again!)

2. The best answer would be a, examples. However, sentences
   2 and 4 are used as a contrast for the two types of vacationers. While b is not the best answer, it is understandable
   why you might pick it.

Try one more practice in (P20) .

 (P20) <u>Practice C</u>

Read the following paragraph. Then answer the questions.

(1) What is transcendental meditation?
(2) It is a technique of meditating developed
by Maharishi Mahesh Yogi which does not involve any form of rigorous mental or physical

control. (3) Likewise, the technique does
not require a devotion to any life style.
(4) It simply consists of two daily sessions
of practice, each for 15 or 20 minutes.
(5) Once in the morning and once in the
evening, the meditator sits in some quiet
spot and thinks only his <u>mantra</u>, a Sanskrit
phrase given to him after initiation.
(6) Through such meditation the meditator
transcends his consciousness and becomes
aware of his unconscious thoughts, hence the
term "transcendental meditation."

1. Which sentence contains the main idea? _____

2. Which of the following best reflects the pattern of relation-
    ships to the main idea? _____

    a. examples/illustration
    b. comparison/contrast
    c. definition
    d. explanation/description
    e. combination

Check your answers in .

---

 1. The main idea is in sentence 1.

2. The best answer is c, definition. The whole paragraph is
    an attempt to define the technique of transcendental medi-
    tation.

Now return to ⑤ if you got here from frame ㊸ . Remember that you got here by means of the check list at the beginning of
this chapter.

If you are finished reading the chapter and you are working your
way through the exercises, go to (P22) .

Practices in Critical Reading

Practice A

Read the paragraph below. Then fill in the blanks which follow.

> A White House staff physician who accompanied President Nixon to China predicted yesterday that acupuncture "just could be the most significant medical rediscovery of modern times and Chinese herbal medicine may prove as important." Speaking at the final scientific session of the American Medical Association's (AMA) 122nd annual convention, Dr. William Lukash urged some 1,000 doctors and other medical personnel to see that there is more clinical research in the United States "to establish acupuncture's true worth before it is put into practice."

1. The author's intent is

   ☐ a. to bring about more study of acupuncture.

   ☐ b. to get the AMA to accept acupuncture.

   ☐ c. unable to tell.

2. The author's attitude toward the subject of acupuncture is

   ☐ a. favorable.

   ☐ b. unfavorable.

   ☐ c. unable to tell.

3. Are you for or against the use of acupuncture as a means of controlling pain? _____ Why? _____

Check your answers in P24 .

 ## Practice B

Read the following paragraph. Then answer the questions.

> No Organic Food Merchant sells white sugar or any products containing white sugar because it is a foodless drug. It is 99.9% sucrose and when taken into the human body in this form is

potentially dangerous. It is touted as an
energy food, but such propaganda is misleading for there is ample evidence that
white sugar robs the body of B vitamins,
disrupts calcium metabolism, and has a
deleterious effect on the nervous system.

1. The author's intent is to call attention

☐ a. to the benefits of eating white sugar.

☐ b. to the harm of eating white sugar.

☐ c. unable to tell.

2. The author's attitude toward his subject is

☐ a. favorable.

☐ b. unfavorable.

☐ c. unable to tell.

3. Do you agree or disagree with the author? _____

Why? _____

Check your answers in (P25) .

---

1. c, unable to tell. The author is reporting, not commenting
on the subject. The quotations and comments which are
pro-acupuncture are not necessarily the author's feelings
or views, but those of the doctor the author cites in his reporting. However, you might have marked a on the grounds
that the author has selected quotes which back up his own
view, but you have no way of knowing that.

2. c, unable to tell. The author has nothing personal to say
about the subject. He quotes what a White House staff doctor has to say about the subject. Again, however, you might
have opted for a for the same reasons as mentioned in 1.
I think that's rather farfetched, but answer keys are not infallible.

3. Answers will vary. Whether you are for or against acupuncture, read both pros and cons regarding the subject before
you make up your mind; that goes for any subject.

Now go to (P23) .

1. b, the harm of eating white sugar.

2. b, unfavorable.

3. Answers will vary but you should always examine the basis
    for your answer. What do you know about white sugar?
    Is your mind open or closed about the subject?

Try one more practice in   .

  Practice C

Read the paragraph below. Then answer the questions which
follow.

> The argument that the death penalty is
> seldom used argues for its retention, not its
> abolition. It proves that juries and courts
> are exercising extreme leniency, even with
> vicious murderers. Yet, there are certain
> heinous crimes regarding which the very
> stones would cry out for the death penalty
> were it abolished. Therefore, it should be
> retained as just punishment and reparation
> for these and as a deterrent for other malig-
> nant criminals.

1. The author's intent is to convince you the death penalty is

    [ ] a. necessary.

    [ ] b. unnecessary.

    [ ] c. against the law.

2. The author's attitude about capital punishment is

    [ ] a. unfavorable.

    [ ] b. favorable.

    [ ] c. uncertain.

3. Are you for or against capital punishment? _____

    Why? _____

Check your answers in (P27) .

1. a, necessary. Notice the last sentence in the paragraph.

2. b, favorable. He is arguing <u>against</u> the idea that because the death penalty is seldom used it should be abolished. He wants to keep it.

3. While answers will vary, make certain your answer is based upon more evidence and reading than is given in this paragraph. Do you have a bias toward or against the death penalty?

Try another practice in .

 Practice <u>D</u>

Below are several statements from prominent magazines, journals, editorials, and speeches. In the blanks in front of the statements, write an F if you think the statement is factual and an O if you think the statement is opinion.

_____ 1. The National Water Commission was created by statute in 1968 to report within five years to the President and Congress as to future national water policy. (<u>Indian Affairs Newsletter</u>)

_____ 2. "Witch doctors and psychiatrists are really one behind their exterior mask and pipe," says psychiatrist E. Fuller Torrey of the National Institute of Mental Health. (<u>Time Magazine</u>)

_____ 3. In addition to their frequently desperate economic plight, working men and women increasingly sense a prejudice against them in academic, intellectual, and liberal circles. (<u>Saturday Review</u>)

_____ 4. The advertisements that describe speed-reading courses try to sound like scientific reports on a major advance in human education, but they are closer to science fiction. (<u>Psychology Today</u>)

_____ 5. In an industrial society nobody is likely to do very well unless he can read, write, and figure very well. (Newspaper editorial)

_____ 6. The book <u>Bury My Heart at Wounded Knee</u> contains a great many errors of fact; some of them are minor, but they add up to considerable misinformation given to the reader. (Book reviewer in historical journal)

(continued)

_____ 7. In the case of World War I, the United States tried hard to keep out of the conflict. But when an imperialistic government in Germany declared an unrestricted submarine warfare on all vessels, including unarmed merchant ships, this was a challenge that could not go unheeded. (History textbook)

_____ 8. Everything you read in this book will help you read better. (Guess who!)

Check your answers in .

---

 1. Fact, not simply because it names names and dates but because the statement is worded in such a way that everything can easily be verified. No opinion is given about the Commission. Of course, if you don't know anything about the Commission then you don't know whether it is fact or fiction. It's one of the hazards of not being well informed.

2. Opinion, as stated. Personally, I agree with the quote, but that doesn't make it fact. As stated, it is an opinion.

3. Opinion. Many working men and women sense no such thing. Beware of generalities such as this one.

4. Opinion, although it makes for a good analogy and this author agrees with the opinion. How about you?

5. Opinion. You may even know some people who do very well and don't know how to read, write, or figure very well.

6. Opinion. However, if the statement can be proven, then it becomes factual. What the author needs to do is prove what he says with examples and proof.

7. Opinion. First of all, there is historical evidence which proves some members of the United States government wanted to become involved in the war. In addition, some historians feel the German U-boat attacks were merely an excuse to become involved in the war. While it is true we did go to war with Germany, the statement itself is not worded in fact.

8. Opinion. Another generality. But it is hoped that most of what—if not all—you read is helpful to you.

Now return to (7) if you are still working in this chapter. Remember, you got here by means of the check list at the beginning of the chapter.

If you finished reading the chapter and are working your way through the practice exercises, you are finished. Go on to Chapter 2.

This concludes the practices in the section on improving comprehension. However, there are more practices dealing with comprehension in Chapter 3.

CHAPTER TWO

Improving Skimming and Scanning Comprehension

GOALS AND OBJECTIVES

General Goals: When you complete this chapter you will be able to:

(1) Recognize the basic writing styles used in newspaper and magazine articles and essays.

(2) Skim read newspaper articles, magazine articles, and essays.

(3) Recognize and use "signal words" to aid your skimming comprehension.

(4) Scan indexes, catalogues, telephone directories, etc., with
more efficiency.

Specific Objectives: When you complete this chapter you will be able to:

(1) Use the basic writing patterns and signal words in newspaper
and magazine articles and signal words to skim read more
rapidly and effectively.

(2) Know when to skim read and when to scan.

(3) Skim and scan read more effectively and selectively.

Sometimes it is not necessary to read every word of an article, newspaper story, or chapter in a book. Your purpose for reading something determines how well you should read it. If you are just browsing for general information, or you merely want to know the high points of an article or chapter in a book, it is not necessary to read the entire work. While skim reading should never be used to replace close, careful reading, it is a useful skill to know and can save you much time when doing research work or looking for quick information.

Good skim reading requires the ability to recognize main ideas and supporting details while reading very fast and skipping over selected parts of whatever is being read. It is necessary for good skimming to have a general awareness of the way different types of reading matter are organized so that you know what to skip and what to read.

Go to ① for a look at how to skim newspaper articles.

---

① Newspaper items generally are printed so that each sentence is a paragraph. This is because columns are narrow and long paragraphs would be solid columns of print. In making each sentence a paragraph, the newspapers provide you with an easy skim reading set-up. In addition, the first sentence of a news story generally gives you a brief summary of the article making it unnecessary to read anything more unless it interests you or you want more detail.

Look at the opening of this news item.

NEW YORK (UPI) — A White House staff physician who accompanied President Nixon to China predicted yesterday that acupuncture "just could be the most significant medical rediscovery of modern times and Chinese herbal medicine may prove as important."

1. Who is the news item about? _____

2. What is the news item about? _____

3. From where does the news item come? _____

4. When did the news occur? _____

5. Why is the item newsworthy? _____

Go to ② .

(2)   If you read carefully you noticed that a lot of information was
gained from one sentence. News items usually follow the predict-
able pattern of stating <u>who</u>, <u>what</u>, <u>where</u>, <u>when</u>, and <u>why</u>. In this
example:

1. <u>Who</u>   a White House staff physician

2. <u>What</u>   the re-discovery of acupuncture

3. <u>Where</u> New York

4. <u>When</u> "yesterday"

5. <u>Why</u>   prediction that the ancient Chinese method may be
"accepted" by modern doctors

At this point you know whether you want to read more carefully or
just skim over the rest of the news story.

Press on to (3).

---

(3)   Here is the opening of another news item. Read it for the who,
what, where, when, and why.

> ST. LOUIS — Mrs. Frank
> Jones, her nine-year-old son
> Bud, and her daughter Sarah,
> burned to death in their bedroom
> when their gas heater apparently
> exploded and flames destroyed
> their home early this morning.

1. Who is it about? _____

2. What is it about? _____

3. Where does it take place? _____

4. When did it occur? _____

5. Why is it newsworthy? _____

Go to (4).

---

(4) 1. Mrs. Frank Jones, her son, and daughter

2. their death by burning

3. St. Louis

4. early this morning

(continued)

5.   Tragedies are always newsworthy.

If you answered all five questions correctly, go to ⑦.

If you missed one or more questions, go to ⑤.

---

⑤   Here is another news item opening. Read it and answer the questions which follow.

> BROOKLYN — Deliberately
> steering his car into the rear of
> a truck when he realized that his
> brakes would not control the car
> in time to avoid hitting a dog,
> John Snopes of Brooklyn was in-
> jured and taken to St. Francis
> Hospital last night.

1.   Who is it about? _____

2.   What is it about? _____

3.   Where does it take place? _____

4.   When did it occur? _____

5.   Why is it newsworthy? _____

Go to ⑥.

---

⑥   1.   John Snopes

2.   crashing his car into a truck to avoid hitting a dog

3.   Brooklyn

4.   last night

5.   It is an unusual cause of an accident; or, all accidents are usually reported when there is hospitalization or death.

Now go on to ⑦.

---

⑦   Reading the opening sentence to a news story is not skimming it. It's a good start but not the end.

If you decide to skim a news story, look for the <u>who</u>, <u>what</u>, <u>where</u>, <u>when</u>, and <u>why</u> in the opening and then let your eyes skip to places where words are capitalized, where numbers appear, or any points which seem interesting to you.   The trick is not to get bogged down in all the words—not, at least, if you are merely looking for high points.

It is easier to tell you to do these things than it is to do them. So try this approach now and see if you can do it.   First, you'll need a watch or clock with a second hand.   Once you have it, go to 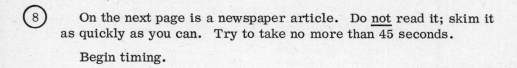 (8) .

(8)   On the next page is a newspaper article.   Do <u>not</u> read it; skim it as quickly as you can.   Try to take no more than 45 seconds.

Begin timing.

White House doctor praises acupuncture

NEW YORK (UPI) — A White House staff physician who accompanied President Nixon to China predicted yesterday that acupuncture "just could be the most significant medical rediscovery of modern times and Chinese herbal medicine may prove as important."

Speaking at the final scientific session of the American Medical Assn.'s (AMA) 122nd annual convention, Dr. William Lukash urged some 1,000 doctors and other medical personnel to see that there is more clinical research in the United States "to establish acupuncture's true worth before it is put into practice."

LUKASH SAID his skepticism turned to "frank amazement when he witnessed major surgery, apparently done successfully, on alert and smiling patients who had only needling to deaden the pain."

But another speaker, Dr. James Y. P. Chen, a member of the acupuncture committee of the National Institute of Health, wrned that the United States should go slow in adopting the medical art practiced in China for 7,000 years.

"THERE IS MUCH to be learned from Chinese medical practices before their achievements, particularly in acupuncture anesthesia, are made reproducible in Western countries,'" said Chen, of Santa Monica.

"Even in China efforts are being made to place acupuncture on a more scientific ground."

David M. Link of the federal Food and Drug Administration (FDA) warned the physicians of "great potential for abuse" if acupuncture continues uncontrolled.

THE ADMINISTRATION ordered last March that all acupuncture equipment be labeled to the effect that it can be used only by licensed medical practitioners.

"Our conclusion was that acupuncture still is in the experimental stage with no demonstrated safe and proper use," Link said, noting that some states already have banned the practice, while others have limited it to physicians and surgeons.

Nevada will license practitioners even if they are not professionals.

MODERATOR of the symposium was Dr. Walter Judd, former Minnesota congressman and onetime medical missionary to China, who said the time was approaching when more state and federal regulation would be necessary to keep acupuncture out of the hands of "fly-by-night" non-professionals who might discredit a valid medical aid.

"I'm glad the AMA has sponsored this meeting to look at the phenomenon of acupuncture coldly and scientifically," Judd said.

"FRANKLY, I have been a little embarrassed because my profession has done little to date to study this practice, out of which can come great benefits. American medical science must find out whether acupuncture is effective and why."

One speaker, Dr. Ronald Melsack, professor of psychology at McGill University, Montreal, challenged the claim that acupuncture does not hurt. He said patients did not want to admit pain and often said they felt "hot" instead.

"It is bearable but painful," Melsack said. "The electrical stimulation hurts and the whirling needle gives a deep, achey feeling."

Stop timing. Record the number of seconds it took to read the article. _____

Now go to ⑨ .

---

⑨   In the spaces below, list any names, dates, places, or points you picked up in your skimming, even if they don't seem to make sense right now. Just list what things caught your eye.

_____

_____

_____

_____

See if you can answer these questions.

1.   What is the White House doctor's name? _____

2.   Where did the doctor make his prediction? _____

    _____

3.   What does the doctor want the AMA to do? _____

    _____

4.   Are all U.S. and Chinese doctors in agreement about acu-
    puncture? _____

Check your answers in ⑩ .

---

⑩   The list of names, dates, places, and points you filled in will have to be checked by looking back at the article and comparing your notes with the actual contents. You might have mentioned the labeling of acupuncture equipment, Nevada licensing practitioners, Dr. Judd, etc. The items should merely reflect what caught your eye. You might even have mentioned things the questions below didn't ask. That's great if you did.

Here are the answers to the questions.

1.   Dr. William Lukash (last name will do)

2.   at the 122nd AMA convention

3.   investigate the true worth of acupuncture

(continued)

4. No, Dr. Chen and Dr. Link warned about accepting it without further study.

If you correctly answered at least three out of the four questions, and took no more than 45 seconds to skim, go to ⑫ .

If you correctly answered two or less, or took more than 45 seconds, go to ⑪ .

⑪   It may take much practice before you become skilled at skimming newspaper stories. The main thing is to keep trying and not give up. There is a tendency for some readers to hold on to every word. Naturally, there are times when you want to do just that. Reading poetry, drama, some sophisticated novels, or philosophy treatises, just to name a few, requires close, careful reading. But that is not the purpose of skimming. Skimming, remember, is a useful technique when you are reading for the highlights, general ideas, or merely looking for something of interest to read.

For the rest of the exercises, skim as fast as you can. You may be surprised at how much you do pick up so quickly. In addition to the drills in this book, practice with newspaper articles in your daily paper. The more practice you do, the sooner you will feel at ease and successful with skimming. If an article looks so interesting you don't want to skim it, you can always go back and read it more closely.

Go on to ⑫ .

⑫   Here is another newspaper skimming exercise. Your purpose is to skim the article on the next page in 45 seconds or less, using what you know about the organization of newspaper stories. Don't start until you have your chronometer (that's a timepiece, friend).

Begin timing.

Noise isn't always something you hear

Noise is not always something you can hear, according to one scientist at Texas Tech University, Lubbock — it is sometimes something you can see.

The scientist is Dr. John F. Walkup, Texas Tech assistant professor of electrical engineering and son of Mr. and Mrs. Frank M. Walker, 190 Cedar Lane, Santa Barbara. And the noise he sees is film grain noise, a pehnomenon that occurs when photographs are electronically enhanced, enlarged or altered to bring out detail.

Photographs are enhanced regularly in fields as diverse as aerial reconnaissance, earth resources satellite surveys and X ray diagnostics. It is essential that the enhanced detail in the photographs be clear and accurate, said Walkup.

"FILM GRAIN NOISE can be a serious limitation in resolving image detail," said Walkup. "The source of the noise is inherent with the nature of film."

He explained that photographic film is usually a sheet of acetate coated with layers of gelatin emulsion containing light-sensitive particles of silver. When exposed and developed, the silver particles from the photographic image.

"Even though the grain structure of a photograph may be invisible to the naked eye, it interferes with the electrical scanning devices which 'read' the photograph during the enhancement process. It can cause distortion in the final form of the enhanced image," he said.

DR. WALKUP is conducting a study to design processors which will produce images of higher quality from images degraded by film noise. The study is financed by a National Science Foundation Engineering Research Initiation grant for $17,000.

Walkup's grant is among 120 Engineering Research Initiation grants awarded young instructors and assistant professors in 73 institutions throughout the United States. More than 780 research proposals were submitted in applications for the grants.

The professor's research includes an investigation of image enhancement techniques which boost the ratio of true image to film grain noise in images produced through the use of various electronic filters. With a research team of graduate and undergraduate students, he is studying possible improvements in the design of the filters used.

Stop timing. Record your time here. _____

Now go to (13) .

(13)   In the spaces below, list any names, dates, places, or points you noticed while skimming even if they don't make sense right now.

_____

_____

_____

_____

Now see if you can answer these questions.

1.   What is the article about? _____

_____

2.   Who is the news item about? _____

3.   From where does the news come? _____

4.   Why is the item newsworthy? _____

_____

Check your answers in (14) .

---

(14)   The list of items you filled in will have to be checked by looking back at the article and comparing your notes with the actual contents. You could have mentioned such things as Dr. John Walkup, Texas Tech University, film grain noise, photographic film, National Science Foundation, $17,000, etc. The items don't have to make sense to you. It merely reflects what caught your eye.

Here are the answers to the questions.

1.   Noise can be seen on film grain as well as heard.

2.   Dr. John Walkup

3.   Texas Tech University, Lubbock, Texas

4.   Walkup received a $17,000 grant to study possible improvements in the design of filters used to record the noise on film.

If you correctly answered at least three out of four questions and took no more than 45 seconds to skim, go to (16) .

If you correctly answered two or less questions, or if you took more than 45 seconds, go to (15) .

(15)   Are you reading instead of skimming and thus taking too long? Are you just sort of "slopping" along? Are you getting interested in the contents and slowing down? Are you afraid you'll miss something? All these things could be holding you back.

Try this the next time:

(1) Read the first sentence carefully.

(2) Read the first part of the second sentence or maybe even all of it if it contains a main point.

(3) Read the first part of each following sentence, but not all of it. If it's a long sentence also read the last two or three words in the sentence.

(4) Read the last sentence.

You may want to move your eyes so that what you see looks something like this:

> Photographs are enhanced
> ...... in fields .... as
> aerial reconnaissance ....
> satellite surveys ... X-Ray ....
> essential .... enhanced detail ..
> photographs .. clear and accurate
> ....

Naturally it was easy to just pick out the key words and print them here and omit the others. But when you skim your eyes should attempt to do just this sort of selected skipping.

For outside practice, take a news item or two in your daily paper and mark out words that are not essential to understanding. A few practices like that might help you do it unconsciously when you skim. It's worth a try.

Better luck next time. Go to .

---

(16)   On the next page is one more news story for skimming. Your purpose is to skim it in 30 seconds or less, using what you know about the organization of newspaper stories. Don't start until you are ready to time yourself.

If you're ready, begin timing.

Gadget nets thieves $500,000 in metals

NEW YORK (UPI) — Thieves with an ultrasophisticated gadget neutralized the alarm system at a precious metal plant in Queens borough yesterday and stole an estimated $500,000 worth of gold, silver and platinum.

Police said the burglars broke through the roof of the L.S. Plate Wire Corp. and then smashed through a concrete vault to get at the precious metals which the firm processed for jewelry, optical, dental and industrial equipment.

THE THEFT was discovered by a representative of Holmes Protection Inc., who entered the shop around 5 a.m. to inspect a "weak" signal being transmitted from the Holmes alarm system there, police said.

The thieves left behind their burglary tools and an apparently homemade electronic gadget that neutralized the alarm system.

"The police said they had never seen such a sophisticated instrument and took it to study it," said an employe who requested anonymity.

"IT WAS about a foot long, three or four inches deep and six inches high with all sorts of wires and dials and stuff," he said.

The employe said the burglars had "left the place a shambles. There's gold and silver dust mixed in with the smashed concrete. It will take a long time to get a complete inventory, but it looks like a half million dollars or more was taken."

THE STOLEN gold was both in six inch bars and powdered, he said.

The firm was broken into about 10 days ago, the employe said, but the alarm went off and the thieves ran before taking anything, he added.

The theft recalled the robbery earlier this year of a lower Manhattan jewelry firm in which all the Holmes alarms in the area were deactivated by thieves who cut the alarm company's main feeder cable.

Record your reading time here. _____

Now go to (17) .

---

(17) Answer the following questions.

1. Who is the article about? _____

2. What is the article about? _____
    _____

3. When did the news take place? _____

4. Where did the news take place? _____

5. Why is the item newsworthy? _____
    _____

6. In what form was the stolen gold? _____

7. What did the electronic "gadget" look like? _____

_____

Check your responses in ⑱ .

_____

⑱   1. thieves with an electronic "gadget"

2. a theft of $500,000 in precious metals from a precious metals plant

3. "yesterday"

4. in Queensborough, New York

5. For two reasons: a theft of one-half million dollars is usually newsworthy, plus the fact that the theft was done with a homemade electronic "gadget" which foiled the plant's alarm system.

6. both six-inch bars and powder

7. a foot long, three or four inches deep, and six inches high with all sorts of dials and stuff. Any close description can be counted as correct.

If you scored five of the seven questions and read in less than

30 seconds, go to ⑳ .

If you scored four or less and read over 30 seconds, go to ⑲ .

_____

⑲   Here are two other methods you might want to practice.

One, use your index finger (that's the one next to your thumb) or a pencil as a guide or pacer and move it down a column of print in an "S" or "Z" pattern, like so:

> Thieves with an ultrasophis-
> ticated gadget neutralized the alarm
> system at a precious metal plant in
> Queensborough yesterday and stole
> an estimated $500,000 worth of gold,
> silver and platinum.
> Police said the burglars broke
> through the roof of the L. S. Plate
> Wire Corp. and then smashed through
> a concrete vault to get at the . . .

(continued)

Your eyes should pick up whatever your index finger is pointing at on each line. It forces you to skip parts and read in groups of words.

Two (if that doesn't work), move your index finger straight down the column. Your eyes will read whole blocks of words but miss the fringe areas on the sides. Your finger acts as a pacer and forces you to read as rapidly as your finger moves.

Try one or both of these methods on some newspaper columns. Don't even worry about what you are reading until you become used to the method. Once you're good at pacing yourself, then concentrate on the content of the article.

At the end of this chapter there are some exercises that may be useful to you if you are having difficulty skimming. Look them over before doing any more frames. Then come back here.

Now go to ⃝20 for a look at how to skim a magazine article.

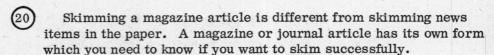

⃝20   Skimming a magazine article is different from skimming news items in the paper. A magazine or journal article has its own form which you need to know if you want to skim successfully.

The first thing to read is the title of the article and the opening paragraph or two. Titles often give you a clue to the author's point and the opening paragraph or two usually state the author's point or thesis regarding his subject.

Next, read only the first sentence of each new paragraph. Usually, each paragraph simply supports or gives examples to support the author's point.

Last, read the last paragraph. It usually contains a summary or conclusion which draws together his points.

Naturally, authors vary their styles and approaches and it may be necessary to adjust these three steps accordingly. However, you will be likely to get more from a skimming method such as this than from just randomly going over the article.

Now go to ⃝21 .

IMPROVING SKIMMING AND SCANNING COMPREHENSION 83

(21)   Check your understanding of what you just read by answering
the following questions.

    1.   The first step in skimming a magazine article is to _____

        _____

        _____

    2.   The second step is to _____

        _____

    3.   The last step is to _____

        _____

Check your responses in (22) .

---

(22)   1.   read (make certain you wrote <u>read</u>) the title and opening
        paragraph or two

    2.   read just the first sentence of each new paragraph

    3.   read (make certain you wrote <u>read</u>) the last paragraph

If you correctly answered all three questions, go to (23) .

If you missed one or more questions, go back to (20) and reread that frame. Then re-do frame (21) .

---

(23)   Here is a short article for you to skim. Remember, this is just
a practice drill, so skim it as rapidly as you can using the technique
explained in (20) . Time yourself and try to take no longer than
60 seconds. The article begins on the next page.

    Begin timing.

THE SUGAR STORY

by Fred Rohe

(1) No Organic Merchant sells white sugar or any products containing white sugar because it is a foodless food. It is 99.96% sucrose and when taken into the human body in this form is potentially dangerous. It is touted as an energy food but such propaganda is misleading for there is ample evidence that white sugar robs the body of B vitamins, disrupts calcium metabolism and has a deleterious effect on the nervous system.

(2) The above material can be concluded by anyone through reading, but in addition to the reading, I have taken the trouble to visit sugar refineries in both Hawaii and California. Aside from general curiosity, my reason for these visits was that I had been selling "raw" or brown sugar without understanding what they are. There was no information available which seemed dependable.

(3) Sugar cane is grown with the use of synthetic fertilizers and weed sprays. The fields are burned just previous to harvest. These are destructive agricultural practices; nothing truly good can come from soil so mistreated. I would, therefore, be uninterested in consuming anything derived from commercially grown sugar cane, either brown sugar or molasses.

(4) Sugar refining is largely a mechanical process done in truly huge machines which boil, spin, filter and separate. Aside from water, the materials which enter the processing are lime, phosphoric acid and diatamaceous earth. I don't consider any of these additives significant where white sugar is concerned because one thing is certainly true about white sugar; it is "pure." No chemical residues could possibly remain at the end of the line, so effective is their purification process.

(5) There are three kinds of sugar which are not white: light brown, dark brown, and Kleenraw. They are all made the same way —by adding back molasses to refined sugar. For years I had heard several different versions of how these so-called "raw" sugars are made. All of them led me to believe that the so-called "raw" sugar which has traditionally been used in the health food industry is a "partially refined" product removed from the refining process some- time before the final stage of white sugar. But my investigation has proved this impression erroneous. All forms of non-white sugars are made from a base of white sugar.

(6) The numbers go like this: Partially re- fined or "raw" sugar is 97% sucrose when it leaves Hawaii and goes through a gigantic Cali- fornia refinery to produce refined sugar, 99.96% sucrose. For Kleenraw they add back 5% mo- lasses, for light brown they add back 12% mo- lasses, for dark brown they add back 13% mo- lasses. A special crystalization process is used for Kleenraw designed especially to create a raw-like illusion.

(7) All sugar companies use similar pro- cesses, as it is against the law to sell sugar which has not been refined. Ostensibly, the pur- pose of this law is to protect us; in reality it means we have no freedom to choose what kind of sugar we would use. Personally, I would like to be able to buy sugar from organically grown cane in the form of an almost black, syrupy mass of crystals. It is rumored that the law which prevents us from buying such true raw sugar was enacted as a result of powerful lobbying on the behalf of the sugar refining companies.

(8) Organic Merchants do not sell brown or "raw" sugar or any products containing brown sugar either, because the plain fact is that brown sugar is a shuck (for those not famil- iar with the term, let's call brown sugar phony).

(continued)

(9) It does not seem to me to be good judgment to ban white sugar because it is refined to the point of foodlessness containing neither vitamins nor minerals, a definite potential human health hazard, and then turn around and sell a product which is made from 87% of the very same white sugar. Having done a thorough personal investigation, I can assure you that brown sugar is nothing more than white sugar wearing a mask.

(10) Besides not liking the 87% part of brown sugar—meaning the white sugar—I don't much like the 13% part either—the molasses. For one thing, the ecologically unsound agricultural practices I mentioned previously; for another thing, those mammoth filtration units the molasses comes out of which are filled with charred beef bones. A representative from one of the sugar companies who came to see me to answer some questions from a letter I had written said the burned beef bones were to give the white sugar a more pleasing "aesthetic" effect. He explained that burned beef bones make white sugar whiter. Of course it's purely personal opinion, but I say God save us from such "aesthetics."

(11) I have not seen Turbinado or Demarara sugar produced, but my understanding of sugar processing enables me to make the following wager with complete confidence: I'll bet Turbinado sugar is at least 95% sucrose. I'm so confident that I would not lose those bets that I won't sell Turbinado or Demarara either. That wager makes no pretense of being founded on "scientific" grounds but on first-hand experience of what sugar looks like during the refining procedure.

(12) Not having known the facts, some Organic Merchants have allowed so-called "raw sugar" to have a home in their stores. Probably, some products containing it are popular. Our intention is not to take the pleasure out of anyone's life, but to play a part in upgrading the quality of American food. If enough of us stop buying junk—even the better junk—the food manufacturers will listen.

(13) So what are you going to use for a sweetener if you never allow sugar to cross your lips? Half the amount of honey should be used in substituting for sugar in recipes. Beyond that, it's all experimental. Try carob molasses, carob syrup, unrefined sugar cane syrup, date sugar. Best experiment of all is to follow the advice of J. I. Rodale: "We receive many letters from readers asking what kind of sugar to use. So far as we are concerned, the answer is none . . . if you would be healthy, omit all sugar and just get accustomed to doing without it."

Record your time here. _____

Go to (24) .

---

(24) Check your skimming ability by answering the following questions.

1. What is the title of the article? _____

2. What is the main idea of the article? _____

_____

3. Sugar cane is grown with the use of synthetic fertilizers and weed sprays. _____ (true/false)

4. There are three kinds of sugar which are not white. _____ (true/false)

5. The author feels that so-called "raw sugar" is the only kind to use. _____ (true/false)

6. What does the author suggest you use in place of sugar?

_____

_____

7. Do you agree with the author? _____ Why?

_____

_____

(continued)

Go to .

 Compare your answers with these.

1.   "The Sugar Story"

2.   White sugar is potentially dangerous to the human body and should not be eaten. See paragraphs 1 and 13.

3.   True; see paragraph 3, first sentence.

4.   True; see paragraph 5, first sentence.

5.   False; see paragraphs 8 and 12.

6.   honey, carob molasses, carob syrups, unrefined sugar cane syrup, date sugar. See last paragraph.

7.   Answers will vary. Your answer should be based on how much you know about sugar, whether the author's "facts" are truly facts, and whether or not you are biased yourself regarding the subject. Now that you've read the article, will you stop eating sugar? Why?

If you correctly answered five of the first six questions, go to .

If you answered four or less of the first six questions, go to .

 If you used the three-step approach discussed in frame (20) , you should have been able to answer the questions. Question 1 asks about the title and question 2 asks for the main idea. Both of these answers are based on the first step in skimming an article; reading the title and first paragraph. Questions 3, 4, and 5 are based on the second step in skimming an article: skim read the opening sentence of each paragraph. Question 6 is based on the last step: read the last paragraph of the article. If you really followed the procedure, you should have been able to answer these questions.

The last question should remind you that critical reading is involved even when skimming. You may be interested in reading the article more carefully and examining the author's facts and opinions. Whatever you answered, make sure it was with an open mind.

Now go to (27) .

(27)   Here is another article for skim reading practice. Use the three-step procedure and skim as fast as you can. Time yourself and try to finish in less than 60 seconds.

Begin timing.

HOUSEBOATING

by Jack Lind

(1) There are basically two types of vacationers. One is compulsive in his determination to throw himself into a whirl of activity. Sometimes his vacations turn into nightmares of physical exertion and mental exhaustion and he's a wreck by the time he gets back to work. He deserves to be.

(2) Then there is the more sedentary type whose thing is slowing down to a snail's pace.

(3) For the latter type I recommend a weekend or a week of houseboating, and it is done no more leisurely than in the Sacramento Delta in Northern California, just 50-60 miles from San Francisco and even less from Sacramento.

(4) After you've landed at either airport, you can rent a car and drive to the delta, or take a bus or fly to Antioch, where one boat rental operator, Gary Carter, will pick up you and your gear. Carter runs Carter's Deluxe Houseboats on Bethel Island, approximately in the center of the delta—a good place to start—and he owns a small fleet of very well equipped houseboats with room for up to 10 people.

(5) I recently rented a 40-foot Kayot Royal Capri houseboat that sleeps 10 and I can't remember when I've spent a more relaxing three days. Houseboating has become a popular pastime in many parts of the country. The

(continued)

boats are large and roomy and they can be
used during a longer period of the year than
most other types of watercraft. Most houseboats cost from $10,000 to $15,000, but fortunately a number of rental operators have gone
into business and you can rent one relatively
inexpensively if you share the cost between
three or four couples.

(6) The one I rented with my wife and two
other couples cost us $150 from noon Friday
to 5 p.m. Sunday, or almost three days. That
comes to a relatively inexpensive $50 per
couple for a three-day weekend, or just $25
per person. And during the off-season, from
September to May, Carter and other operators
offer a 20 percent discount.

(7) For the money, you get a large boat
with all modern conveniences, including elec-
tricity, refrigerator, stove and hot water
shower in the bathroom. Our boat came with
dishes and silverware, pots and pans, mattresses
and deck chairs and a small dinghy. It's the
most comfortable floating hotel I've ever been in.

(8) You bring your own supplies, fishing
tackle, food and drinks. For our first dinner
we roughed it with filet mignon with bordelais
sauce, asparagus tips with hollandaise, cheese
and fresh fruit with a couple of good bottles of
wine—but you are welcome to go anyway you like.
The cooking facilities are excellent on board.

(9) Piloting a houseboat is disarmingly
simple; after a one-hour orientation course
and perusal of a delta chart, any Girl Scout
can handle the controls. The fact that most
houseboats will go no faster than 7-8 miles an
hour makes the reflexes of a race car driver
quite unnecessary.

(10) The main secret to navigating in the
Sacramento Delta, I discovered, is to follow
the charts carefully. There are more than
1,000 miles of meandering waterways throughout the 480 or so square miles of delta country
and it is very easy to get lost unless you mark
your route and follow the chart closely.

I strongly recommend against night boating
for novices—they might find themselves in-
extricably lost. (In the daytime, of course,
you can always ask advice from passing river
boats. There's a good deal of slow-paced
traffic over the major arteries in the delta.)

(11) Houseboating is an exhilarating experience if you have attuned yourself to
chugging through several days at 8 m.p.h.

(12) The delta consists of innumerable
little islands and inlets laced with sloughs
and canals. Behind the dikes and levees that
shore up much agricultural land you may find
grapevines, blackberry thickets blooming
white and golden poppies. In the autumn,
Mount Diablo, looming high above the flatland
in the background, turns gold and lavender.

(13) Fishing is good in the delta, both with
light and heavy tackle; in fact, some say it is
one of the best fishing areas on the Pacific
Coast. In the spring there's a heavy run of
striped bass, in the fall there's salmon and
steelhead and in some spots (ask around)
you're apt to find black bass. There's also
plenty of catfish, crappie and bluegill and in
a few areas you may get a chance to tackle a
huge sturgeon.

(14) If you are a fisherman, be sure to buy
a state fishing license (it costs $3). The people
of the California Fish and Game Department
sometimes come alongside in their big grey
boats, yell at you through bullhorns to produce
a license and then inspect it through high-
powered binoculars.

(15) One of the great things about houseboating in the Sacramento Delta is the tranquility
and the absolute privacy. The bigger boats are
roomy enough for everybody aboard to do his
own thing—a big sundeck on top, an aft deck for
a little trolling, a fore deck for a game of cards
or liar's dice, plenty of bunk space for napping
and a small boat for excursions or visits on land.

(continued)

(16) The land is flat, but there's plenty
to see and many areas to visit. Much of it
can be reached only by boat—towns like
Walnut Grove, where they used to have gam-
bling dens and where they still have an old
Chinese burial ground (it was largely Chinese
labor that built the levees). Or Locke,
Isleton and Terminous. Some of them have
overnight accommodations, but who needs it
with a houseboat? There are plenty of marinas
and stores for supplies and bait on the way.

(17) There is, in season, even a good deal
of social life and a fair amount of saloons and
restaurants along the way. Among the more
elaborate facilities are those around Ehrich's
Fishing Resort and Lost Isles, a 40-acre island.
The owner, Bill Conner, a former Lipton soup
salesman, runs a nice restaurant and bar from
April to January and, incidentally, plays a
mean gutbucket. Tiki Lagun, which is nearby,
is another nice watering hole and dining spot.

(18) There are a number of old drawbridges
crossing the waterways. A houseboat will go
under most of them while they are closed. In
one case, however, we thought we couldn't make
it and honked at the bridge tender. Normally,
he comes out on his bicycle and operates the
bridge. But we didn't honk three times as river
etiquette demands—and besides, he could plainly
see that we could make it, so he ignored us.

(19) The Sacramento Delta is made up of a
confluence of the Sacramento, the Mokelumne and
the San Joaquin Rivers and in older days the waterways were the main channels of transportation
for gold miners and their equipment. Today, a
few large barges and freighters still ply the waterways, but there is enough water around to prevent
traffic jams.

(20) In some areas the water is brackish;
nevertheless some people enjoy swimming in the
delta and there are some very nice beaches, including one at Lost Isles.

(21) Houseboating in the Sacramento Delta has become so popular that it is smart to make reservations well in advance, especially during the summer months. The rental operators will be glad to help you plan your trip.

(22) It's worth every penny of the price.

Record your time here. _____

Go to (28) .

(28) See how well you did by answering the following questions.

1. What is the title of the article? _____

2. What is the author's main idea? _____

_____

3. The author went houseboating for four days.

_____ (true/false)

4. The cost of renting a houseboat was $150.

_____ (true/false)

5. Piloting a houseboat is tricky business, according to the author. _____ (true/false)

6. The author went houseboating

☐ a. along the Mississippi River.

☐ b. in Walnut Grove Lake.

☐ c. near the Sacramento Delta.

7. Fishing is good only with light tackle. _____ (true/false)

8. Which one of the items below best describes the author's attitude about houseboating?

☐ a. enthusiastic

☐ b. humorous

☐ c. impartial   (continued)

9. There are a number of _____ crossing the waterways.
    a. islands
    b. drawbridges
    c. channels

10. It is best to get reservations if you go houseboating where the author did. _____ (true/false)

Check your answers in (29) .

---

(29) 1. "Houseboating"

2. Houseboating is a relaxing, leisurely vacation. See paragraph 3.

3. False; see paragraph 5, first sentence and paragraph 6, first sentence.

4. True; see paragraph 6.

5. False; see paragraph 9.

6. c, near the Sacramento Delta; see paragraph 10, first sentence, paragraph 19, first sentence, and paragraph 21, first sentence.

7. False; see paragraph 13, first sentence.

8. a, enthusiastic. His use of "enthusiastic," "one of the great things," and "worth every penny of the price" are all clues.

9. b, drawbridges; see paragraph 18, first sentence.

10. True; see next to last paragraph, first sentence.

Considering each question to be worth 10 points, making 100 possible points, if you scored 70% or better and skimmed in less than 60 seconds, go to (32) .

If you scored 60% or less, go to (30) .

---

(30)   If you skimmed in 60 seconds or less and answered 50 percent of the questions, you're not doing too badly. It's not great, but it's not bad. Skimming, remember, is not careful reading. Therefore, whatever you get from skimming in the way of information you didn't know before is a gain.

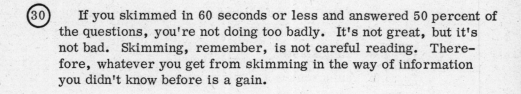

It is suggested that you skim back over the questions you missed, check the places in the article where the answers appear, notice that the questions all come from places in the article you are supposed to skim and analyze your errors.

When you understand where you "goofed," go on to ㉛.

㉛ Check your knowledge about skimming magazine or journal articles by listing the three-step procedure in your own words.

1. ____________________

____

2. ____________________

____

3. ____________________

____

Check your answers in ㉒. Then go to ㉜.

㉜ It is also possible to apply skim reading techniques to textbook reading; however, this subject is covered in Chapter 4 where study reading skills are discussed. You'll learn more about it there.

For now, go on to ㉟.

㉝ This is just a little note to let you know you aren't supposed to be here and to caution you against looking for frame ㉞ because there is none.

Get quickly to ㉟.

㉟ Scanning is similar to skimming in that you use the reading technique when it is not necessary to read something in its entirety. But unlike skimming, you use scanning when you know in advance what you are looking for. For instance, when you want to look up a word in a dictionary under the H's, you don't read every word listed under the H's. You scan, using alphabet clues to lead you to the right page. Likewise, when you want to see if there are tires to fit your car listed in the Sears catalogue, you skip the sections

(continued)

with dresses, dishes, tools, and toys and look under the automotive section.

You already know how to scan. You use it every time you use a phone book, an index, or a movie listing in a newspaper. But in all cases, you <u>know</u> <u>in</u> <u>advance</u> what it is you are looking for and ignore what is not useful. That is one of the basic differences between skimming and scanning.

Go to (36) .

---

(36)   In the space below, write a statement which defines scanning and when you use it.

_____

_____

_____

Go to (37) .

---

(37)   Your statement should contain the fact that (1) scanning, like skimming, is a reading technique which is useful when you don't have to read everything in its entirety, and (2) that it is used when you know in advance what you are searching for.

If your answer contained these two points, go to (38) .

If your answer was not correct, go back to (35) and reread the explanation and try (36) again.

---

(38)   On the opposite page is a page from the index of a textbook. Use it to see how well you can scan. Is your watch or clock still handy? You'll need it again to time yourself.

Using the index page, scan it and find the page reference listed for Pierre Auguste Renoir. Time yourself to see how long it takes you and then return here to record your time and your answer.

Begin timing.

Record your time. _____

Record your answer. _____

Go to (39) .

(39)   Your answer should be page 499 and your time should have been less than 20 seconds.

If you did this correctly, go to (41) .

If you had trouble, go to (40) .

---

(40)   The first thing you should have noticed about the index is that it lists mostly R's and some S's. Since indexes use last name listings, you should have let Renoir be your guide. Scanning down the column you should have used Ren, the first three letters in the name, as your guide. Once you found Ren, you should have used the next letters in the name, oi, as your guide until you find Renoir. Since the name appears near the top of the first column, it should have taken you very little time.

Go to (41) .

---

(41)   Using the same index page and scanning technique, find the first page reference listed for the Russo-Japanese War and record your findings in the spaces below.

Begin timing.

Record your time. _____

Record your answer. _____

Go to (42) .

---

(42)   The answer is page 566. Your time should be no more than 20 seconds.

If you did this correctly, go to (44) .

If you had trouble, go to (43) .

---

(43)   Your guide letters this time were Russ. You should have quickly read the first word in each column to serve as guide words. Since column two begins with Rom, it is obvious Russ would not be in the first column. This leads you directly to column two. Moving to the second column, you should have easily located the listing for Russia. It sticks out pretty plainly because of all the listings under it. That should have let your eyes drop down from all the listings under Russia to the next major listing, Russo-Japanese War.

Go to (44) .

---

(44)   Try another one. Timing yourself, scan for the <u>last</u> listing for Rumania and the First World War. Then return here to record your time and answer.

Begin timing.

Record your time. _____

Record your answer. _____

Go to (45) .

---

(45)   The answer is page 611. Your time should have been under 20 seconds.

If you did this correctly, go to (49) .

If you had trouble, go to (46) .

---

(46)   You may have had trouble because the question asked for the last listing and you may have noticed only the first page listing. Since Rumania had several listings, it was necessary for you to look first for Rumania, then scan for First World War.

Go to (47) .

---

(47)   Try one more. You probably have the index page memorized by now, but the practice will do you good. Timing yourself, look for the page listings for the Italian Renaissance and record your results here.

Begin timing.

Record your time. _____

Record your answer. _____

Go to (48) .

---

(48)   The answer is pages 56-65. Your time should have been under 20 seconds.

Go to (49) .

(49)   You can develop your scanning skills by practicing with the index in this or any other book, by selecting some words and looking them up in the dictionary, by using the TV Guide and looking up your favorite programs, by looking up your friends' names in the telephone directory, and numerous other ways you can think of if you put your mind to it and need it. If you don't need it, then forget it and use your time on something more profitable.

Go to (50) .

---

(50)   Sometimes, when doing research or reviewing before a test, you can use scanning beneficially. For the sake of practice and learning, let's say that you were talking to a friend about the article on sugar you skimmed earlier. Since you only skim read it, you don't remember all the facts but your friend wants to know if the article mentions anything about Turbinado sugar and, if so, what it says.

Return to frame (23) and scan the article for any mention of Turbinado sugar. Read what it says and return here when you are finished.

Go to (23) now.

If you scanned the article, use the space below to write what is said about Turbinado sugar.

_____

_____

_____

_____

Now go to (51) .

---

(51)   The article mentions that Turbinado sugar is probably produced in the same manner as regular sugar, though the author personally has not seen it refined. He bets that it is 95 percent sucrose and does not believe it is any better than white sugar. Your answer should have covered these points. It's all in paragraph 11 of the article.

Now go on to (52) .

(52)　　Let's pretend again. This time pretend you have been talking to your physics teacher about the article on noise sometimes being something you can see. Your physics instructor wants the name and address of the man who is doing the experiments on the project. You promise you can get it for him.

Return to (12) and scan the article for the name and address of the man conducting the experiments. When you have finished return here.

Go now to (12) .

If you have finished, use the space below to write the name and address you located.

_____

_____

Now go to (53) .

---

(53)　　The man's name is Dr. John F. Walkup, Assistant Professor of Electrical Engineering, Texas Tech University, Lubbock, Texas. If you wrote the Santa Barbara address given, you scanned too rapidly. That address belongs to his parents. However, if you had trouble with this it could easily be because the article is confusingly written and not a fault of your scanning.

If you feel you understand the scanning process and need no more practice, go to (58) .

If you feel you need more practice, go to (55) .

---

(54)　　The answer is Dr. Ronald Melsack. The answer is found in the next to last paragraph, in case this one gave you trouble.

Go to (57) .

---

(55)　　Here's another practice drill. Return to frame (8) and scan the article on acupuncture for the name of the doctor who challenges the claim that acupuncture does not hurt. Come back here when you have found the answer.

Go to (8) now.

(continued)

If you found the answer, write it here. _____

Go back to (54) .

---

(56)   The answer, L. S. Plate Wire Corp., is found in the second paragraph.

Now go to (58) .

---

(57)   Try one last drill. Go back to frame (17) and scan for the name of the company that was robbed of $500,000. Come back here when you have the answer.

Go to (17) now.

Write your answer here. _____

Go back to (56) .

---

(58)   This concludes the unit on skimming and scanning.

The following practice exercises are useful for developing rapid word and phrase perception, something necessary for efficient skimming and scanning.

PRACTICE EXERCISES FOR DEVELOPING
SKIMMING AND SCANNING TECHNIQUES

The following exercises are not programmed, but rather they are grouped
into sets. It is best if you do only one set of exercises in each practice
session. They are designed to help you speed up your perceptual ability,
that is, your ability to see key words and phrases correctly. As other
drills in this chapter, they should be timed.

Set I

Exercise 1

Directions: Below are two columns of phrases. Together, the phrases
make no sense so do not attempt to read for comprehension. The object
is to read down the two columns and to check the phrase in summary
every time you see it in either column. You should finish the exercise
in less than 20 seconds.

Begin timing.

like this one	never before
not right now	in summary
in all respect	in essence
for the time	in demand
in summary	not for now
in the summer	over the bridge
write a summary	in summary
a raw-like one	in surveys
they add to	on the road
in the end	in summary
in summary	just go now
from a base	to produce it
light brown	from the top
when it leaves	in the book
before the final	my white coat

Record your time. _____ (20 seconds is average)

The phrase in summary appears five times. Count the number of
phrases you marked.

Exercise 2

Directions: Some words signal the reader that more of the same idea is going to be presented. For instance, the word furthermore indicates that the author is going to keep on supporting the same point, as in the sentence "You can't go today; furthermore, you can't go tomorrow, either."

There are three lists of words below. Circle all the words you think signal the reader that more of the same type of idea is going to be presented. Time yourself.

Begin timing.

also	therefore	furthermore
never	likewise	more than that
but	again	accordingly
however	sometimes	essentially
moreover	and	in addition
necessary	carefully	concluding

Record your time. _____ (25 seconds is an average score)

You should have marked also, moreover, likewise, again, and, furthermore, more than that, in addition. All of these signal that the author is going on with more of the same.

Exercise 3

Directions: Underline the phrase greatly needed every time it appears in the group of words below. Time yourself.

Begin timing.

> greatly concerned   not before now   from this
> moment   greatly needed   beside the lake
> group of words   garage mechanic   greatly
> needed   on Sundays only   near my heart
> greatly needed   some other time   count me out
> greatly needed   try it again   book titles   it is
> necessary   tell me later

Record your time. _____ (15 seconds is average)

You should have marked greatly needed four times. Check your markings.

Exercise 4

Directions: There are two lists of names on the next page. Check or mark all the famous ones you have heard or read about.

Begin timing.

Tom Jones
Cyril Abbot
John Smith
Nancy Drew
Dana Smith
Anthony Newley
Robert Redford
Lee Kennedy
James Stewart
Carl Shutz

Sam Ervin
Frank Sinatra
Winston Churchill
Fred Green
Jack Lips
Dave Longhorn
Winnie Shad
Herb Alpert
Harry Lime
David Dunn

Record your time. _____ (20 seconds is average)

Answers will vary. Check to make certain you marked all the names you meant to mark.

Exercise 5

Directions: Practice skimming straight down a newspaper column of your choice. Time yourself three times on the same column, trying to outdo yourself each time.

Practice 1. _____ seconds

Practice 2. _____ seconds

Practice 3. _____ seconds

If you came here from frame (19) , return there now.

If you are working your way through the practice exercises, take at least a 12-hour break and then go on to the next set. Set II begins on the next page.

Set II

Exercise 1

Directions: Mark the key phrase <u>heart's content</u> every time it appears in the columns below. Time yourself.

Begin timing.

the measure was	blindness is
heart's content	right to burst
heavy container	heart's content
justice itself	contented heart
the same time	same as before
heart's broken	would result
heart's content	the attitude of
another warning	widely known
it may not	heart's content
handle this	has been seen
heart's content	never mind
broken into	such a deal
scores more	hearts beat
damaged heart	heart's content
his attitude	liquid fuel

Record your time. _____ (20 seconds is average)

The phrase <u>heart's content</u> appears six times. Count the number of phrases you marked.

Exercise 2

Directions: Some words signal the reader that a change of ideas is about to occur. For instance, the word <u>nevertheless</u> indicates that the author is going to change his point, as in the sentence "I believe I am right and he is wrong; nevertheless, I may be mistaken."

In the list of words below, there are several words such as <u>nevertheless</u>, which can be used to signal an author's change in view. Circle all those words.

Begin timing.

also	likewise	rather
more	despite	essential
but	accordingly	yet
so	however	nevertheless
thus	summarily	carefully
although	eccentric	moreover

Record your time. _____ (25 seconds is average)

You should have marked <u>but</u>, <u>although</u>, <u>despite</u>, <u>however</u>, <u>rather</u>, <u>yet</u>, <u>nevertheless</u>.

Exercise 3

Directions: Underline the phrase <u>reading comprehension</u> every time it appears in the group of words below. Time yourself.

Begin timing.

> The entire paragraph   never before
> from here to there   reading comprehension
> near the building   reading skills   poor
> comprehension   reading comprehension
> guide the way   reading concentration   reading
> comprehension   greatly needed   swim for
> miles   buy it now   see the light   don't bother
> me   reading comprehension   several more
> is this the way   read and study   reading skills

Record your time. _____ (15 seconds is average)

You should have marked <u>reading comprehension</u> four times. Check your markings.

Exercise 4

Directions: There are two columns of book titles below. Mark all the ones that begin with B. (Don't count the word "The.")

Fail-Safe   Black Elk Speaks
The French Lieutenant's Woman   Catcher in the Rye
Couples   Stranger in a Strange Land
Bech: A Book   The Man Who Killed the Deer
The War Lover   The Seven Minutes
Love Story   The Great Gatsby
To Kill a Mockingbird   Deliverance
Ship of Fools   Vanity Fair
The Brothers Karamazov   Crazy Horse
The Thin Red Line   Steppenwolf

Record your time here. _____ (15 seconds is average)

You should have marked <u>Bech: A Book</u>, <u>The Brothers Karamazov</u>, <u>Black Elk Speaks</u>.

Exercise 5

Directions: Practice skimming straight down a newspaper column of your choice. Time yourself three times on the same column, trying to outdo yourself each time.

Practice 1. _____ seconds

Practice 2. _____ seconds

Practice 3. _____ seconds

Compare your time with Exercise 5 in Set I.

Set III

Exercise 1

Directions: Mark the key phrase <u>public relations</u> every time it appears in the columns below. Time yourself.

Begin timing.

rent a car	the latter type
share the cost	popular pastime
you and me	public relations
public service	between three
with my wife	your gear
public relations	more sedentary
from noon on	he's a wreck
public rooms	public relations
public relations	public utilities
in the center	for the day
more relaxing	a few large
public relations	in some areas
slowing down	pony express
with a room	etiquette demands
the whole one	public relations

Record your time. _____ (20 seconds is average)

The phrase <u>public relations</u> appears six times. Count the number of phrases you marked.

Exercise 2

Directions: Some words signal the reader that a summary or conclusion is about to be stated. For instance, the word <u>therefore</u> signals that a final point is to be made, as in the sentence "Therefore, I feel we should vote yes."

In the list of words below there are several words like <u>therefore</u>, which can be used to signal an author's summary or conclusion is about to occur. Circle all those words.

Begin timing.

also	again	consequently
more	thus	furthermore
moreover	despite	accordingly
so	therefore	in addition
but	rather	in summary
although	however	in conclusion

Record your time. _____ (25 seconds is average)

You should have marked <u>so</u>, <u>thus</u>, <u>therefore</u>, <u>consequently</u>, <u>accordingly</u>, <u>in summary</u>, <u>in conclusion</u>.

Exercise 3

Directions: Underline the phrase <u>rental operators</u> each time it appears in the group of words below. Time yourself.

Begin timing.

> A popular pastime   during a longer
> from now on   rental operators   you can find
> can be used   large and roomy   rental operators
> too nice for it   rent is due   rental operators
> three-day weekend   on my time   a number of
> them   rental operators   more than most
> buried within   large and roomy   tell me more
> some time this year   rental operators   that's
> all for now

Record your time. _____ (15 seconds is average)

You should have marked <u>rental operators</u> five times. Check your markings.

Exercise 4

Directions: Scan the paragraph which follows and circle all the two-letter words which appear in the paragraph. Time yourself.

Begin timing.

(continued)

Houseboating has become a popular pastime in many parts of the country. The boats are large and roomy and they can be used during a longer period of the year than most other types of watercraft. Most houseboats cost from $10,000 to $15,000, but fortunately a number of rental operators have gone into business and you can rent one relatively inexpensively if you share the cost between three or four couples.

Record your time. _____ (20 seconds is average)

You should have marked nine words. Check your markings.

Exercise 5

Directions: Practice skimming straight down a newspaper column of your choice. Time yourself three times on the same column, trying to outdo yourself each time.

Practice 1. _____ seconds

Practice 2. _____ seconds

Practice 3. _____ seconds

Compare your time with Exercise 5 in Set II.

Set IV

Exercise 1

Directions: Mark the key phrase complete confidence every time it appears in the columns below. Time yourself.

Begin timing.

complete chaos	largely mechanical
complete confidence	purification process
complete overhaul	complete confidence
complete honesty	especially easy
overly confident	syrupy mass
coming thing	overly concerned
complete hatred	complete confidence
complete account	our intentions
organically grown	seal your lips
overly refined	beyond all that
refining companies	concerned with
complete disaster	complete confidence
complete confidence	would be true

Record your time. _____ (20 seconds is average)

The phrase <u>complete confidence</u> appears five times. Count the number of phrases you marked.

Exercise 2

Directions: In previous exercise sets you identified signal words such as <u>therefore</u>, <u>however</u>, <u>thus</u>, <u>but</u>, and <u>moreover</u>. Time yourself while you scan the group of sentences below and check all the signal words you see.

Begin timing.

> I want to go, consequently I will try my best. Moreover, I intend to make certain that my calendar is clear that day. Despite my busy schedule, I will work something out so that I will be free. However, I will need your cooperation also. Although I feel I can trust in your judgment, I would appreciate clarification from you. In summary, look for me there.

Record your time. _____ (25 seconds is average)

You should have marked <u>consequently</u>, <u>moreover</u>, <u>despite</u>, <u>so</u>, <u>however</u>, <u>although</u>, <u>in summary</u>.

Exercise 3

Directions: Underline the phrase <u>synthetic fertilizers</u> each time it appears in the group of words below. Time yourself.

Begin timing.

> Rental conditions   operating procedures
> the wrong time   never on Saturdays   symphonic
> music   large waterfalls   synthetic fertilizers
> scheduled ahead   synthetic parts   sucrose in
> large parts   aside from water   consider
> synthetics   confident of gains   science first
> symbols of gold   the above material   that's
> all folks

Record your time. _____ (15 seconds is average)

You should have marked <u>synthetic fertilizers</u> once. Check your marking.

Exercise 4

Directions: Scan the paragraph below and circle all the three-letter words which appear in the paragraph. Time yourself.

Begin timing.

> Sugar cane is grown with the use of syn-
> thetic fertilizers and weed sprays. The fields
> are burned just previous to harvest. These
> are destructive agricultural practices; nothing
> truly good can come from soil so mistreated.
> I would, therefore, be uninterested in con-
> suming anything derived from commercially
> grown sugar cane, either brown sugar or mo-
> lasses.

Record your time. _____ (20 seconds is average)

You should have marked the, use, and, The, are, are, can. Check your markings carefully.

Exercise 5

Directions: Practice skimming straight down a newspaper column of your choice. Time yourself three times on the same column, trying to outdo yourself each time.

Practice 1. _____ seconds

Practice 2. _____ seconds

Practice 3. _____ seconds

Compare your time with Exercise 5 in Set III.

This concludes the practice exercises for this chapter.

CHAPTER THREE
Improving Speed of Comprehension

GOALS AND OBJECTIVES

General Goals: When you complete this chapter you will be able to:

(1) Identify how many words per minute you can read with good comprehension based on various purposes in reading.

(2) Recognize an author's purpose, his attitude toward his subject, and his use of supporting details.

(3) Adjust your rate according to your reading purpose.

(4) Define the terms "speed of comprehension," "regression," and "mind wandering" as related to reading.

(5) Write a brief statement about what you read.

Specific Objectives: When you complete this chapter you will be able to:

(1) Read with better speed of comprehension.

(2) Read for the author's main ideas, his attitude toward his subject, and his use of supporting details.

(3) Draw inferences about what you read.

(4) Eliminate faulty eye movement, regression, and vocalization from your reading.

(5) Condense what you read into a brief statement or summary.

"I took a speed-reading course, learning to read
straight down the middle of the page, and I was
able to go through <u>War</u> <u>and</u> <u>Peace</u> in twenty minutes. It's about Russia."

Woody Allen

You, too, can learn to read <u>War</u> <u>and</u> <u>Peace</u> in twenty minutes. And
you'll get about the same comprehension that Woody Allen claims. However, the object of reading is usually to acquire knowledge, information,
or to experience entertainment. Since it is more important to be able to
talk about <u>what</u> you read than to talk about <u>how</u> <u>fast</u> you read, the term
<u>speed</u> <u>of</u> <u>comprehension</u> will be used here. No matter how many words
per minute your eyes can read, you can only comprehend as fast as your
mind can absorb the ideas being read.

A good reader is a flexible reader according to: (1) his needs or purposes for reading (discussed in Chapter 1), (2) his background of information on the subject, (3) his vocabulary knowledge, and (4) the difficulty
of the reading material. The purpose of this chapter is to help you develop
your maximum flexibility in reading speed of comprehension.

You've probably heard about people who supposedly can read thousands
of words per minute. Don't you believe it. Some people are able to develop a high proficiency of skimming or scanning at a thousand or so
words per minute, but according to research, it is impossible to read,
as most of us think of reading, more than about 900 words per minute.
The human eye just can't handle speeds higher than this without skimming
or skipping. If you have worked in Chapter 2 already, you know that you
can skip much and still comprehend some of what you are reading, but
that technique is used for special purposes.

It is usually rather easy to double your average reading rate simply by
consciously trying to read faster than you normally do. At first, because
you are thinking about reading faster, you may lose some comprehension.
However, that's because your mind is more concerned with increasing
your rate, not comprehension. That's perfectly natural and no cause for
alarm. Soon, after two or three practice sessions, your comprehension
should catch up with your rate. This means that you could read most
materials in half the time it takes you now.

Some readers are afraid to try reading faster. They are convinced
that they will misread or not understand what they are reading. Conse-
quently, they continue to read at the old, comfortable, safe speed. Nothing much can be done for readers with this attitude until they are willing
to sacrifice some comprehension in practice sessions. The sacrifice
soon pays off, however, once they give it a try.

There is only one way to increase your speed of comprehension—practice daily. In this chapter, several timed reading selections are provided for your use in improving your comprehension. Each article is followed by comprehension exercises. The questions test your ability to use what is presented in Chapters 1 and 2—setting a purpose for reading, recognizing main ideas and supporting details, separating fact from opinion—and, something new, drawing inferences. Drawing inferences simply means making a conclusion about something the author believes from certain things he says or his attitude toward his subject.

The answers provided for the questions on comprehension are designed to help you learn from any mistakes you may make on the questions. When you make a mistake, learn from it by checking on the reason for your error. It may even be that you are correct and the answer is wrong or ambiguous.

Improved comprehension cannot occur at the snap of your fingers. It requires time, practice, and a willingness to learn from mistakes you may make. The exercises in this chapter are not important by themselves, but taken together with the others in this book they will have a role in the total effect on your reading comprehension. It is also recommended that you do not attempt to do more than two timed reading selections in one day. Space them out by working in other sections in the book or by practicing the techniques described in this chapter.

Reading Record Chart

Timed Readings	Comprehension Score (%)	Rate (WPM)
Selection 1		
Selection 2		
Selection 3		
Selection 4		
Selection 5		
Selection 6		
Selection 7		

The chart above should be used to keep a record of your reading rate (WPM = words per minute) and comprehension score. You are competing against yourself. Try to do better on each reading selection. If you truly learn from your mistakes, you will see your progress on the chart and, more importantly, feel the benefits in your everyday reading.

Now go to ①.

---

①   Once more you are going to need a watch or a clock with a second hand so that you can time your reading speed. If you have one, go to ②. If you don't, go get one and come back to ②.

---

②   Timed Reading Selection 1

Don't start this drill unless you have a watch or clock.

You are going to time yourself while you read from the following selection, "Hot Dog!" It is not difficult to read and the subject matter is no doubt familiar to you.

Your purpose:

    (1) read as rapidly as you can and still understand what you reading

    (2) look for the author's thesis or main point

    (3) look for any facts, figures, or ideas he uses to support his thesis or main point

    (4) don't try to remember everything, only those points mentioned above

If you have completed Chapter 1, all this is old stuff to you. This exercise gives you a chance to use that information. If you haven't read Chapter 1, you may want to work in it after you see the results of this exercise.

Check your watch or clock and write down your starting time when you begin reading. Start exactly on the minute. It will make it easier to figure your reading rate (WPM).

Starting time. _____

Begin reading.

HOT DOG!

(1) "As American as apple pie," people say, but they might well say "As American as a hot dog." Think of July Fourth, flags and baseball games, and the ubiquitous frankfort-and-roll invariably enters your mental image. The ordinary hot dog occupies a special place in America's history and tradition.

(2) Americans named the hot dog. We made it famous all over the world and we even managed to make it fashionable. But the original didn't arrive here until 1872, long after the Austrian and German versions of the hot dog were popular in Europe. The first American vendors weren't quite sure how to handle and serve hot dogs. They tried serving them directly from the grill to the customer's hands, and it became painfully evident that they were too hot to handle.

(3) Something had to be done, so white gloves were lent to the customers while they ate. But people tended to wander off with the gloves and it became too expensive. The hot dog might not have become the great success it did, if it weren't for an enterprising soul with another solution.

(4) His name was Antoine Feuschtwanger and he was a sausage peddler in St. Louis. He knew he had a big opportunity to sell hot frankforts at the great St. Louis World's Fair, so he devised the first baked-to-fit roll. The combination of frankfort and roll brought the hot dog its first measure of solid popularity.

(5) The name "hot dog" and the arrival of the pleasing little weiners on the American sports scene came in 1900. The Giants were playing at New York's Polo Grounds on a chilly day, and the ice cream and soda pop weren't

(continued)

selling well. The gloomy concessionaire
suddenly remembered Feuschtwanger's
popular combination and decided to sell it
as a cold-weather food from then on. He
equipped his vendors with portable hot water
tanks to keep the sausages and rolls hot.

(6) The cries of "Get your red hot dachshund sausages" were heard by newspaper
cartoonist Tad Dorgan. Legend has it that
Dorgan quickly realized the comic cartoon
potential of a barking sausage but, like many
of us, couldn't seem to spell "dachshund."
So he drew a cartoon and dubbed the character
"Hot Dog" instead. The name stuck, and so
did the association with sports, with the result that today few bleacherites are unfamiliar
with the reassuring call of "Hot Dog!" A hand-
ful of nourishment is always within easy reach.

(7) Who are the champion hot dog eaters?
Many people would vote for baseball fans, who
regularly provide the press with stories of
prodigious appetites. Take a recent game between the Phillies and Giants on a hot, humid
day in Philadelphia, for example. Some say
it was so humid that the pitchers could have
been throwing spitballs and the umpires wouldn't
have noticed. At any rate, fans were fainting
all over the stands and the first aid stations
were jammed. And what was business like at
the food stands? Booming. What was the top-
selling item? You guessed it—hot dogs—a full
ton and a half of them before the last fan had
left the park.

(8) Hot dogs have come a long way socially
since the summer day at Hyde Park in 1937
when Eleanor Roosevelt shocked her husband's
very proper mother (and much of the world) by
treating George VI and the British royal family
to a typical American menu that included the
humble sausages. High society now regards hot
dogs as "in," and they make the international
gossip columns regularly. In recent months
they have been mentioned along with champagne
at a famous author's discotheque party, again

at a $30-a-ticket charity gala sponsored by
a top fashion magazine, and at a Riviera
bash attended by European royalty. Nor has
hot dog's appeal diminished as a plain, all-
American food. Grilled frankforts and rolls
continue to rate high in popularity with customers at Howard Johnson's restaurants
from Maine to California. Everyone from
the visiting statesman to the campaigning
small town politician uses the hot dog to
create a friendly, folksy image in this country.
A few years ago even Nikita Khrushchev posed
with this capitalist snack and described it as
"wonderful."

(9) Hot dogs are favored with baked beans
and in dozens of other dishes, but some purists
maintain that the only perfect hot dog is one
served in a roll topped by one or a combination
of the following: mustard (the favorite), pickle
relish, ketchup, chopped onions, sauerkraut
and chili sauce. How big is a hot dog? The
average measures about 5 1/2 inches in length,
3/4 inches across and weighs about 1 1/2
ounces. Travel around, however, and you'll
discover sizes designed to be gobbled in a single
bite and "foot-long" extravaganzas.

(10) The largest hot dog made in the U.S. was
so big (17 feet long, 80 pounds in weight) that it
required a tractor and trailer to haul it along
with its tailor-baked bun to the Michigan scene
of its unveiling.

(11) Most hot dogs consist of beef, pork,
sugar, salt, spices and sodium nitrate. Meat
is chopped, cured, spiced, encased, linked,
smoked and cooked before it is weighed,
wrapped and shipped to stores and restaurants.
Skinless franks are molded in a seamless,
transparent, edible cellulose tube.

(12) The end product is a delicious combination of nourishment, fun and American
tradition. Breathes there a man with soul
so dead, who never to a vendor has said,
"Gimme two with mustard and relish!"

Record your reading time here. _____

Now go to ③ .

---

③ Answer the following questions without looking back at the article.

1. The main idea of the author is to

☐ a. discuss the origin of the hot dog in America.

☐ b. show that everybody eats hot dogs in America.

☐ c. show the place the hot dog has in American tradition.

2. The author's attitude toward his subject is

☐ a. favorable.

☐ b. unfavorable.

☐ c. unable to tell.

3. The hot dog originated in the U.S. _____ (true/false)

4. Hot dogs were first served in America with

☐ a. sauerkraut.

☐ b. bread.

☐ c. white gloves.

5. The first hot dog bun was introduced to the public

☐ a. at a Giants baseball game.

☐ b. by street vendors.

☐ c. at the St. Louis World's Fair.

6. The name "hot dog" came from a cartoon with a barking frankfurter. _____ (true/false)

7. The hot dog was introduced to "high society" when

_____ shocked her mother-in-law by offering frankfurters to the King of England.

8. Hot dogs are gaining popularity in other parts of the world but losing their popularity in the U.S. _____ (true/false)

9.   The largest hot dog made in the U.S. was

☐   a.   16 feet long, 70 pounds in weight.

☐   b.   17 feet long, 80 pounds in weight.

☐   c.   18 feet long, 90 pounds in weight.

10. The hot dog, the author says, is a delicious combination
of nourishment, fun, and American tradition. This is a

statement of _____. (fact/opinion)

Check your answers in ⑤.

---

④   You're not reading very carefully. You were told to go to ⑤.

---

⑤   1.   c; while the author does discuss the origin of the hot dog and
makes a case for the popularity of the hot dog, he does so
to show the place the frankfurter has in American tradition.
Answer a is too narrow; answer b is not true because not
"everybody" likes hot dogs; answer c is stated in the opening paragraph.

2.   a; it certainly is not an unfavorable report on the hot dog.
The fact that he has done some research on its history, calls
the hot dog as "American as apple pie," and relates that
high society even likes hot dogs shows his favorable attitude
toward the subject.

3.   False. It originated in Europe. See paragraph 2.

4.   c; see paragraph 3.

5.   c; see paragraph 4.

6.   True. "Get your red hot dachshund sausages" didn't have
the ring to it that "hot dog" has. See paragraph 6.

7.   Eleanor Roosevelt. See paragraph 8.

8.   False. At least, nowhere in the article is this stated.

9.   b; see paragraph 10.

10. Opinion. While you may think so and the author may think
so, the statement itself is opinion. To some, hot dogs are
not delicious. To health food eaters the hot dog is taboo because it is full of sodium nitrate and left over meat scraps.
And for others, eating hot dogs is not their "idea of fun."

(continued)

Go to ⑥ .

---

⑥   Count the number of correct responses you made on the comprehension check and multiply the number correct by 10 to arrive at your percentage, or amount earned out of 100 possible points. For instance, six correct answers would be 60%.

        Comprehension score. _____

Now subtract your starting time from your finishing time to see how many minutes and seconds it took you to read the article. Use the space below.

        Finishing time. _____

        Starting time. _____

        Total reading time. _____

Use the chart below to figure out how many words per minute you read. Use the number of minutes and seconds listed below which comes closest to your time and then circle your WPM. For instance, if you read for 4 minutes and 20 seconds, you rate would be 222 WPM because it is closest to 4:30.

Time	WPM	Time	WPM
1:00	1000	5:30	181
1:30	667	6:00	167
2:00	500	6:30	154
2:30	400	7:00	143
3:00	333	7:30	133
3:30	286	8:00	125
4:00	250	8:30	117
4:30	222	9:00	109
5:00	200	9:30	100

Record your Comprehension Score and your WPM for Selection 1 on the chart on page 115. Then return here.

If your comprehension score was 70% or more, go to ⑧ .

If your comprehension score was 60% or less, go to ⑦ .

---

⑦   Based on the scores of 250 community college freshmen, 60% or less is just a little bit below their average on this material, but it's nothing to worry about at this point. In fact, it is possible that you might do even better on a different set of questions about the article. Often, you might understand what you read very well, but not do well on some questions because of the way they are worded, because tests might make you nervous, because you misread the test questions, or a dozen other reasons. So don't be discouraged by the test scores at this point.

If you have not read Chapter 1, you may wish to do so before contintuing in this chapter. There you will receive some information about comprehension that may help you in this chapter.

If you decide to continue, the best thing you can do for yourself is to make certain you understand why you missed the questions you did. The answer key tells you where to find the correct responses to the questions you missed. Reread those paragraphs indicated in the answers and decide whether you misread the question or the article or just didn't remember what you read the first time. Making yourself conscious of what you are doing wrong helps you to overcome the problem.

Doing this for each question you miss will begin to have a positive effect on your overall comprehension. You will begin to automatically pay attention to points or ideas that you otherwise might have missed.

When you have finished analyzing your mistakes on the comprehension quiz, go to ⑨ .

---

⑧   Nice work. Based on scores of 250 college freshmen, the average comprehension score is about 70% on this selection. You're doing fine in the comprehension department. In fact, if your WPM was low (222 WPM or less), you can afford to practice reading faster on future drills. Try it, you'll like it!

Go on to ⑨ .

---

⑨   If your rate for Selection 1 was 250 WPM or more, go to ⑪ .

If your rate for Selection 1 was 222 WPM or less, go to ⑩ .

---

⑩   The average WPM for Selection 1, according to test scores of other college freshmen prior to any reading training, is around 250 WPM with 70% comprehension. Your WPM is below average. However, at this point it may not be significant, especially if your comprehension score was 70% or better. On the next timed reading

(continued)

selection, cut loose and read as fast as you can. You may just be shy about reading rapidly.

If both your WPM and comprehension score were low, you should work first on bringing up your comprehension score. Once it becomes "average," begin raising your rate score.

Go to ⑫ .

---

⑪   Good show! The average rate for college freshmen without reading training is around 250 WPM with 70% comprehension. Your reading rate was average or better.

If your comprehension was average or better with this rate, you're in good shape. Try harder next time! Your potential may be way up there.

If your comprehension was low, then you may be reading too fast. However, you were told to read fast and if your comprehension dropped, don't worry about it now. Keep your eye on those comprehension scores and if they don't start going up, then you may need to slow down. But for now, keep practicing at rates faster than you're used to.

Go to ⑫ .

---

⑫   There are a few common habits many readers have which often keep them from reading at faster rates of comprehension. See if any of these apply to you.

Vocalization, or the sounding out of words by moving your lips when you read silently. (This is discussed in Chapter 1.) If you form the sound of each word as you read silently, you will not read much faster than you can talk, which is not much over 100 words per minute. Vocalization is not a sin, but it is certainly a "no-no" if you want to read faster. As mentioned in Chapter 1, reading with a pencil held between your lips will help you to stop the habit of moving your lips because you will soon get tired of that pencil falling out!

Regression, or rereading the words on a line you already read. This is not to be confused with purposely rereading something because it wasn't clear the first time. Regression is an unconscious habit of retracing your eyes over what you are reading. This habit is analogous to walking down the street and suddenly walking back the way you came, then going forward again, then backing up, and so on. Naturally, such a walk would take you longer to get where you are going. It's the same in reading. You may lose up to a fourth of your reading time just regressing. As you do future reading exercises, force yourself to keep your eyes moving from left to right without regressing on any line.

Mind wandering, or daydreaming as you read instead of getting involved in the reading matter. Mind wandering usually occurs when the material is uninteresting or there is no purpose for reading that is meaningful. Overcoming mind wandering is usually done by establishing purposes for reading and by getting involved in the subject matter.

Ignoring unknown words, or failing to develop your word knowledge. Without a plan to develop your vocabulary, as covered in Chapter 1, you cannot expect to develop your comprehension powers. Comprehension comes from knowing not only the meaning of the words you read, but how the author uses them to convey his meaning and attitude. If you know now that you need to develop your vocabulary, return to Chapter 1 and work through the frames dealing with that.

As you work through this chapter, be aware of these common habits that readers develop. If you need help in overcoming these habits, see the practice exercises at the end of this chapter, beginning on page 177.

Now go to ⑬ .

---

⑬   Timed Reading Selection 2

Don't start this selection unless you have a watch or clock with a second hand.

Time yourself while you read from the following selection, "Motorcycling Gains New Image."

Your purpose:

read as rapidly as you can and still understand what you are reading.

You are testing yourself for your speed of comprehension so do not get bogged down in minor details or descriptions. That is not your purpose here. Instead, look for what the author feels is a "new image" for the motorcycle.

(continued)

Remember: Don't vocalize.
Don't regress.
Don't daydream.

Write down your starting time. Start exactly on the minute.

Starting time. _____

Begin reading.

MOTORCYCLING GAINS NEW IMAGE

(1) Motorcycling, once a special interest that was associated with fringe groups and eccentric personalities, has become the basis for a thriving motorsport, a popular middle-class pastime and a burgeoning industry within the past two years. Direct correlations between rising trends in motorcycle racing and sales have traced the spiraling success of a sport capturing the interest of a growing number of Americans.

(2) Following a sales slump in 1967 and 1968 created in part by mandatory helmet-use laws and introduction of compact automobiles, the motorcycle business bounced back in 1969 and began a geometric increase that developed into a one billion dollar industry in 1971.

(3) Doubling between 1960 and 1965, then again between 1965 and 1970, motorcycling has become the interest of well over 12,000,000 Americans, recognized by President Nixon in an Executive order of February 8, 1972. The figure is expected to increase in 1973, reflecting the steadily heightened interest in the hobby.

(4) The versatility of the vehicle seems to be part of the reason for its growing popularity. Motorcycles now may be anything from a mini-bike built especially for a six-year-old up to a powerful, streamlined road machine capable of comfortable freeway

cruising. Motors range from 50 cubic centimeters up to 1200 cubic centimeters,
amounting to more power plant than many
small Italian cars possess.

(5) With more people riding motorcycles,
the quantitative change reflected in the public
mind by the demise of the image of the motorcycling outlaw. Middle and upper class Americans have taken to motorcycling as a means
of convenient transportation and recreation,
diminishing the social impact of the renegade
rider by sheer force of numbers.

(6) A survey commissioned by the American Motorcycle Association in 1971 indicated
that the average family income of motorcycle
enthusiasts exceeded $13,000 a year as com-
pared to the national average family income
of slightly over $8,000. In addition, more
than 77 percent of motorcyclists in the United
States have completed high school and 50 percent are married, indicating that the average
is much higher than most non-motorcyclists
realize. Though associated with youthful
activities, the motorcycle hobby is populated
by users averaging 30 years of age.

(7) Cutting the cloth for the new image
are such Hollywood personalities as Steve
McQueen, Ann Margret, James Garner and
Dick Smothers. McQueen, famous for his
exciting motorcycle scenes in "The Great
Escape," is in fact an accomplished motorcyclist who has been featured on the cover
of Sports Illustrated for his competitive
exploits on motorcycles.

(8) Famous figures in the worlds of
business, high finance and politics who ac-
tively pursue motorcycling are General
Motors' Bill Mitchell, Malcolm Forbes of
Forbes Magazine and Doug Toms, President
Nixon's director of highway safety under the
Federal Department of Transportation.

(9) Along with the growth of the industry
and its change of image have come larger

(continued)

race purses, spiraling attendance figures and the entry of motorcycling into prestige race tracks across the United States.

(10) As a motorsport, it blends equal quantities of man and machine more than in any other sport utilizing the internal combustion engine. Fans develop a strong interest in racing personalities since the rider is always foremost in the spectator's gaze. Whether on the heavy, powerful machines tailored for road courses or on the light, agile motorcycles used for cross-country competition, the rider himself is never enshrouded by metal or machinery. Perched on the seat of his vehicle, he shifts, brakes and accelerates in full view of the spectator.

(11) In terms of pure athletics, motorcycling excels over other motorsports. Machines range from 200 to 300 pounds, sometimes possessing a power-to-weight ratio of nearly a horsepower per three pounds. Brute strength, dexterity and athletic skill often play a major role in operating a machine of such high power and low overall weight.

(12) Medical tests made on world championship riders under competitive conditions show that for physical exertion motorcycling is surpassed only by soccer, according to the American Motorcycle Association.

(13) The largest motorcycle organization in the world, the American Motorcycle Association is one of the oldest sports sanctioning bodies in the United States. Originating in 1903 as the Federation of American Motorcyclists, the AMA incorporated under its present name in 1924. In 1927, its headquarters moved from Chicago to the Columbus, Ohio area, where it remains today.

(14) The AMA is a race sanctioning body as well as a membership service organization, governing nearly all aspects of the sport. Its current membership, approaching 200,000, dwarfs other major sports organi-

zations. It is also the sole United States affiliate to the Federation Internationale Motorcycliste, world governing body for the sport.

(15) As a membership service organization the AMA provides basic insurance policies for members, legislative direction on a national level, televised spots promoting motorcycle safety and a major monthly publication on the sport.

(16) Chartered clubs number nearly 2,000 and follow suggestions of a Community Relations Kit designed to make them respected and active organizations in their communities.

(17) The AMA sanctions and conducts most of the motorcycle competition in the United States, including amateur and professional racing as well as land speed record attempts. During 1973 more than 1,500 professional and 7,000 amateur events will be sanctioned by AMA and supervised by its officials. Types of activity include all forms from amateur trials and enduro riding to the highly professional AMA National Championship Circuit.

(18) The AMA has made a concentrated effort to upgrade its competition during the past two seasons. Success in 1971 was marked by single payoffs reaching more than $100,000 and entrance into the most prestigious tracks in the nation.

(19) The AMA governs championship racing on both pavement and dirt. In road racing, such tracks as Daytona, Talladega, Ontario and Laguna Seca are sites of professional motorcycle competition, and on the dirt AMA riders circle the finest horse tracks available.

(20) Championship events in 1972 paid over $500,000 in purses, and additional manufacturers' contingencies made a total of $1,200,000 available to championship motor-

(continued)

cyclists. Topping the list were a 200-mile
road race at Daytona International Speedway in March and a 250-mile road race at
Ontario Motor Speedway in October, each
offering the riders about $100,000 in purses
and contingencies.

(21) This year the purses will climb
along with spectator interest. Crowds increased at every event on the championship
trail in 1972, and they are expected to do
so again in 1973. Annually more than 65,000
fans witness two championship events in
Houston's Astrodome, and in March Daytona
International Speedway draws more than
50,000. AMA predicts that by October the
26-event championship series will have been
followed by more than a half-million fans.

(22) Focus of the personality-oriented
spectators are top professionals from 16 to
38 years of age. Topping the list in age and
achievement is Dick Mann, 38, of Richmond,
California, twice AMA Grand National Champion. Mann was on the championship circuit
when some of his competitors were in kinder-
garten. His first time to carry the prestigious
Number One plate was in 1963.

(23) In contrast, a fellow Californian,
Kenny Roberts, earned a national championship license at the age of 20. He was the
nation's top novice rider at 18, became the
top junior the following year and began his
first week as an expert by winning a national
championship event.

(24) Men of this caliber sometimes find
motorcycling to be a good training ground for
auto racing. Examples are Mike Hailwood,
who currently holds a contract to drive for
John Surtees after having won a string of
world motorcycle championships, and US-AC
star Joe Leonard, who won the AMA Grand
National Championship three times. As a
motorcyclist, Leonard won 27 individual
championship events.

(25) Next for this transition appears to be 1970 Grand National Champion Gene Romero. Acclimated to speed after five years on the AMA championship circuit, Romero qualified to race on the high banks of Pocono the first time he ever drove a stock car.

(26) Mecca for motorcycling racing enthusiasts is Daytona Beach, where the annual motorcycle classics are held every March. Daytona hosts one of the oldest annual events in motorcycling history, and a part of the longstanding tradition is the social life centering around the Holiday Inn located directly across the street from the famous speedway.

(27) As with many of the major tracks on which AMA racing stars perform, Daytona's Inn is conveniently positioned as a kind of headquarters where America's new breed of motorcyclists and motorcycle enthusiasts gather to chat, renew old friendships and speculate on the weekend's bill of exciting motorcycle competition.

Finishing time. _____

Now go to ⑭ .

⑭   Answer the following questions without looking back at the article.

1.   The main idea of the article is that

   ☐ a. motorcycle sales are higher than ever before.

   ☐ b. motorcycles are more versatile than ever before.

   ☐ c. motorcycles are growing in popularity.

2.   The author's attitude toward his subject is

   ☐ a. humorous.

   ☐ b. serious.

   ☐ c. neutral.

(continued)

3. The number of Americans interested in motorcycling in 1972 is reported as

☐ a. 12 million.

☐ b. 14 million.

☐ c. 16 million.

4. One of the reasons given for the rise in popularity of the motorcycle is its versatility. _____ (true/false)

5. A survey done by the AMA shows the average age of motorcycle users is

☐ a. 25.

☐ b. 30.

☐ c. 35.

6. Which of the following was not listed among popular personalities interested in motorcycling?

☐ a. Steve McQueen

☐ b. Ann Margret

☐ c. Ryan O'Neal

7. Along with the growth of the motorcycling industry, interest in motorcycle racing has also increased. _____ (true/false)

8. Medical tests made on world championship cycle riders show that for physical exertion motorcycling is surpassed only by basketball. _____ (true/false)

9. The statement, "The AMA is a race sanctioning body as well as a membership service organization, governing nearly all aspects of the sport" is a statement of _____. (fact/opinion)

10. The reader can infer from the article that the author received most of his information for the article from the American Motorcycle Association. _____ (true/false)

Check your answers in ⑮ .

1. The best answer is c. It is true that motorcycle sales are higher than before and motorcycles are more versatile, but both are due to the growth in popularity. If you still don't buy c, then reread the title of the article and look at paragraph 1 and the first sentences of paragraphs 2, 4, 5, and 9.

2. b. Most of the article is based on straight reporting of statistics on motorcycling.

3. a. This question is just one of literal recall, that is, remembering the figure the author reported. It is not a particularly important piece of information, but it fits in as a supporting detail regarding his main idea and you should have been aware of his use of the detail to back up his point. See paragraph 3.

4. True. See paragraph 4. This you should have remembered because it is one of the reasons given to support his main idea about the popularity of motorcycling.

5. b, 30. See paragraph 6. This is another supporting bit of information given to show the changing image of the motorcycle. Always let your mind register those points which an author uses to support his main ideas.

6. c, Ryan O'Neal. See paragraph 7. Don't feel too badly if you missed this question. It's typical, though, of the type of questions reading tests generally ask. It's simply a test of recall and not really related to the purpose you were given for reading.

7. True. See paragraph 9. A good deal of the article dwells on this interest, the amounts of money involved, the track locations, and winning personalities.

8. False. It's soccer. See paragraph 12. This, too, is a test of your recall ability and not of major importance as a question.

9. Fact. It can be verified by checking the AMA charter and purpose.

10. True, or at least it's a good guess. Paragraphs 12 through 27 are loaded with references to the AMA. If the author didn't, he certainly makes it look that way to the reader.

Now go to 16 .

(16)　　Count the number of correct responses you made on the comprehension check and multiply the number correct by 10% as you did for Selection 1.

Comprehension Score. _____

Then subtract your starting time from your finishing time to see how many minutes and seconds it took you to read the article. Use the spaces below.

Finishing time. _____

Starting time. _____

Total time. _____

Use the chart below to figure how many words per minute you read. Use the number of minutes and seconds listed below which comes closest to your time and circle your WPM.

Time	WPM	Time	WPM
1:00	1400	5:00	280
1:30	933	5:30	254
2:00	700	6:00	233
2:30	560	6:30	215
3:00	467	7:00	200
3:30	400	7:30	186
4:00	350	8:00	175
4:30	311	8:30	165

Record your comprehension score and WPM for Selection 2 in the chart on page 115. Then go to (17) .

---

(17)　　If you scored 60% or more, go to (19) .

If you scored 50% or less, go to (18) .

---

(18)　　As mentioned earlier in this chapter, paying attention to your mistakes is the only way to automatically increase your powers of comprehension. Try to analyze the type of errors you are making. For instance, which questions are you tending to miss—main idea, attitude, fact/opinion, recall, or inference? Look again at the questions you missed and determine if there is a pattern to them. Remember, too, there are practices in this type of comprehension development in Chapter 1, and if you haven't done them, it might be worthwhile to give them a try.

Keep in mind that the answer key here may provide answers that are arguable. You may have good reason or arguments for a different answer from the one furnished. Don't sell yourself short. The main thing is to pay attention to <u>why</u> you answered as you did and learn from the answer comments.

Go to ⑳ when you have finished analyzing your mistakes.

---

⑲ A score of 60-70% or better is very good for the type of questions asked on this article. You're doing fine. Chances are that you can even experiment a little and try reading a bit faster than you are. On the next timed reading selection, experiment with a little faster reading speed and see what happens. If you can learn to double your reading rate of comprehension, you would have time to read twice as much or to take longer coffee breaks!

Go to ⑳ .

---

⑳ By now you have the speed of comprehension results for two timed reading selections (three if you have completed Chapter 1). You should have a fair idea of your reading power for average material. Reading experts claim that the national norm for high school graduates is about 250 WPM with about 60-70% comprehension. How do you compare with this claim?

Reading, like any other skill, requires practice in order to be developed fully. If you are interested in increasing your speed of comprehension, you must decide to spend at least half an hour or so each day "in training." Here are some training exercises or "reading calisthenics" you can use to help yourself.

(1) Get a 3 x 5 card or something like it and as you read a newspaper or magazine article, use the card to force yourself to read faster by covering up the lines as you read. In other words, use the card as a pacer so that you just barely finish reading the last word on the line before the card covers it. This is a speed drill to help you overcome regression tendencies and to force you to read faster than you normally would. Do this for about five or ten minutes per day as a warm-up exercise, without worrying about comprehension. It's an eye movement drill.

(continued)

(2)   Practice the "S" or "Z" method of skim reading you were introduced to in Chapter 2, by working through the practice exercises which begin on page 177.   Again, don't worry about comprehension; the method is an eye exercise which helps you use your peripheral vision— vision surrounding the actual focal point of your eyes.

(3)   Read a short news item or magazine article as rapidly as you can without falling into a skimming technique. Then, without looking back, put into your own words, either orally to someone or on a piece of paper, what you just read.

(4)   After you have practiced doing the above, read something of interest to you at your normal pace.   Chances are it will be faster than usual and you won't even be aware of it.

Do these exercises every day for the next three weeks.

Now go to ⃝21 .

⃝21   Be sure you don't develop the habit of ignoring words you don't know.   Scan back through the article and jot down any words you don't know or words which may have caused you to misread something because you didn't know the meaning.   Make vocabulary cards for them as mentioned in Chapter 1, or work on learning the Greek and Latin word lists in that chapter.   Remember, better comprehension is often the result of a better vocabulary.

Go to ⃝22 . . . tomorrow.   Right now, take a break for at least 12 hours.   Don't ever do more than two timed readings in one day.

⃝22   Timed Reading Selection 3

Don't start this selection unless you have a watch or clock.

Time yourself while you read the following article, "Easy Rider." No, it isn't another motorcycle article—but you're close.

Your purpose:

(1)   Read as rapidly as you can and still understand the author's main idea and attitude toward his subject.

(2)   Don't get bogged down in details or technical description.

(3) Don't vocalize.

(4) Don't regress.

(5) Don't let your mind wander.

Check your watch or clock and write down your starting time when you begin. Start exactly on the minute.

Starting time. _____

Begin reading.

EASY RIDER

by Steve Goldstein

(1) The call of the wild was nothing compared to the call of the 10-speed racing bike. As I stood there with my nose pressed against the plate glass of the bicycle shop, I could think of ten reasons why I had to have one. Aside from the fact that bicycling is fantastic exercise, this was my one great chance to do something for ecology. Besides, I knew how sexy I'd look bent over those fancy handlebars.

(2) The scene inside the shop was chaotic: people milling around German, Italian, English and French bikes stacked to the ceiling. At the counter, young and middle-aged customers were plunking down hundred dollar bills.

(3) I'd read up a little on the subject before I got here, and I didn't want the kid behind the counter to think I was your average biking novice, the kind who didn't know a sprocket cluster from an Ashtabula crank. When my turn came, I told him I wanted the $250 "Silver Monarch" Deluxe, with all the extras on it, too. He wasn't impressed. I quickly gathered that putting accessories on the Silver Monarch would be like drawing arms on the Venus de Milo. Mirrors and kickstands and raccoon tails fastened to the

(continued)

handlebars were now taboo. Speed was everything with a 10-speed. In fact, the more you
paid, the less you got.

(4) Three days later I put on the uniform
of the biking fraternity for the grand exit
through my lobby. My polo shirt had a series
of pockets spread across the front where I
could keep cookies and assorted spare parts.
I had fancy $8 gripping gloves, and I'd bent
back the brim of my racing cap in the accepted
fashion, even though it made me look like an
itinerant house painter.

(5) The Silver Monarch had maes-type
handlebars—another addition to my growing
bike vocabulary. The maes bar had several
basic advantages over the "all-rounder,"
which was the kind you'd always seen on
every other bike. Maybe that was its main
advantage. I wasn't sure. The part you
gripped with your gloves swept over and down.
To reach front and rear hand brakes you had
merely to keep your thumbs hooked into the
bar and grope fiercely upwards with the rest
of your fingers.

(6) Outside, perched on my bike at last
and fighting the wobblies, my body arched
forward almost in a sprint, I managed to ride
for several minutes—until my neck gave out.
You see, the strain has to go somewhere, so
the body cleverly shifts the cramp from the
leg muscles through the back region and into
your neck. To distract myself, I decided to
try out the levers that put the bike through
each of its ten speeds. For the uninitiated,
I'll quickly explain this efficient mechanical
principle.

(7) The left-hand lever found on the front
down tube of your bike controls a cable on
the jockey roller of the rear derailleur (also
called a spindly-armed changer). Moving it
through its five positions will feed the chain
into any of five different gear ratios strung
along the freewheel cluster. Switching the
right-hand lever backwards and forwards

will nudge your front derailleur from a large-toothed sprocket to a smaller, second one. Two times five is ten. Simple, isn't it?

(8) Unfortunately, the manufacturer does not point out the hazards of shifting directly from the highest high to the lowest low. The first indication that something was wrong came when I heard a loud "ker-plunk." Then I noticed that my drive chain had fallen off. Mishaps such as this are easily remedied by patient finger work, and in no time at all, smiling to myself, I aligned the chain with twenty-four of the teeth on the front sprocket.

(9) Remounted, my confidence growing, I headed for a rural parkway a few miles away. At a crowded intersection, I felt smug as I glided between lanes of horn-blaring autos.

(10) My complacency was short-lived. One of the drivers opened his car door abruptly. He caught me square between the stem and front fork, and I fell over hard.

(11) My doctor tells me the broken ankle is coming along beautifully, and being a fellow bicycling enthusiast, he's provided me with a list of secluded country lanes. You can reach the nearest one by car in an hour. He even said I could borrow a spare bike rack for the Silver Monarch.

(12) I haven't the heart to tell him I sold it.

Record your finishing time here. _____

Go to (23) .

(23) Answer the following questions without looking at the article.

1. The main idea of the article is

☐ a. the author has given up bike riding.

☐ b. the hazards of bike riding.

☐ c. the author's experience at bike riding.

2. The author's attitude toward his subject is one of

☐ a. seriousness.

☐ b. humor.

☐ c. indifference.

3. The author says he could think of ten reasons for buying a ten-speed bike, but only gives three. Name at least one.

_____

4. Which bike did the author buy?

☐ a. the Schwinn Deluxe

☐ b. the Silver Monarch Deluxe

☐ c. the Venus de Milo

5. Describe the shirt the author wore the first time out on his new bike. _____

6. How long did the author ride before his neck got tired?

☐ a. several minutes

☐ b. several hours

☐ c. several miles

7. What happened when the author tried out his ten speed gears?

_____

8. The author gives a brief lesson on how the gears of a ten-speed bike work. _____ (true/false)

9. Describe how the author broke his ankle. _____

_____

10. What does the title "Easy Rider" have to do with the subject of the article? _____

_____

_____

Go to ㉔ .

㉔ Check your answers with these.

1. c. It isn't a even though the author has given it up. It is because of the experiences he had that he gave it up. While he does discuss the hazards he encountered personally, he does not discuss as his main point the hazards of bike riding.

2. b, humor. It's doubtful you missed this one, but if you did, take another look at the opening paragraph where he describes himself with his nose pressed against the bike shop window, his comment on how sexy he'd look on a bike, his description of buying bike—all are related with a sense of humor.

3. Look in paragraph 1. He gives three reasons: bicycling is "fantastic exercise," it's good ecologically, and he knew he'd look sexy on a racer. Any one of these three is correct.

4. b; see paragraph 3.

5. It was a polo shirt with pockets for spare parts and cookies. See paragraph 4.

6. a; see paragraph 6.

7. The chain came off. See paragraph 8.

8. True. See paragraph 7.

9. He was driving between cars and someone opened their car door as he passed. See paragraphs 9 and 10.

10. Answers will vary, but you might draw a parallel between the motorcycle heroes of the movie "Easy Rider" compared with his humorous account of himself as a cool, sexy bike rider. The word "easy" has a slang connotation meaning "cool." There is humor in his attempt to become a cool, "with it" bike rider. Or, the fact that he quit bike riding after his first time out because bike riding for him was not easy is another play on the title. Give yourself credit if your answer relates to those offered here.

Go to ㉕ .

㉕ Count the number of correct answers and multiply by 10%.

Comprehension Score. _____

(continued)

Subtract your starting time from your finishing time to determine your total reading time. Use the spaces below.

Finishing time. _____

Starting time. _____

Total time. _____

Use the table below to figure your WPM. Find the number of minutes and seconds closest to your reading time and circle your rate.

Time	WPM	Time	WPM
1:00	750	3:30	214
1:30	500	4:00	187
2:00	375	4:30	162
2:30	300	5:00	150
3:00	250	5:30	138

Record your comprehension score and WPM for Selection 3 in the chart on page 115. Then come back here.

If your WPM was 250 or over, good work! Go on to (27) .

If your WPM was 214 or less, go to (26) .

(26) A rate of 214 WPM is not necessarily bad, but it is not particularly a fast rate considering your purpose was to read as rapidly as you could and still understand what you were reading. The article is short, not full of facts or points which your mind needed to register, and you were told to ignore any technical facts or details. Therefore, a rate of 250 WPM or better on this article is considered average or better.

Remember that these drills are just that—drills. Feel free to read faster than you normally do. If you make mistakes, make them here, not on your "outside" readings. Practicing includes making mistakes, so "hang loose" and push your rate a little more.

Reading speeds will vary with length of articles, the difficulty of the material, your purpose for reading, and your background of information you are able to bring to your reading. Rate is not really important, although it may sound like it here. But don't read everything at the same rate or at a slower rate because it is "comfortable" or your habit to do so. On future drills, try reading faster. If you really don't understand what you read at faster rates, then maybe you have already reached your maximum potential. But you'll never know unless you try.

Move along to .

 Just another reminder that you should be improving your vocabulary through the vocabulary card method, the memorization of Greek and Latin root words, or a vocabulary book of your choice. It's necessary if you want to develop comprehension. Work on vocabulary now. Then go to (28) .

---

(28) Timed Reading Selection 4

Don't start this exercise unless you have a watch or clock.

Time yourself as you read the following selection, "Requirements: Aid or Deterrent to Education?"

Your purpose:

(1) Read rapidly, looking for the author's answer to his own title question.

(2) Don't vocalize.

(3) Don't regress.

(4) Don't let your mind wander; read fast.

Write down your starting time when you begin reading. Start on the minute.

Starting time. _____

REQUIREMENTS: AID OR
DETERRENT TO EDUCATION?

by Orvel E. Hooker

I have some educational suggestions to make.
(1) Declare at least a one year moratorium on the use of all textbooks. Most of them are boring, poorly written, and almost all of them assume that knowledge exists prior to, independent of, and altogether outside of the learner. Let the student write his own text-

(continued)

book. This would be a real contribution to education.

(2) Cross professors over their fields of specialization. Let someone from the Humanities teach Chemistry and Math and someone from the Sciences teach English Literature and Philosophy. Let the Social Sciences do what they want to; they usually do anyhow.

(3) Require every professor who thinks he knows his subject to write a book on it. Should he do so, he would probably stop telling his students how much he knows and they might learn something.

(4) Abolish all "subjects," "courses," and "requirements." This proposal alone would wreck the existing educational establishment. We could start all over and teachers could no longer give excuses for their failures.

(5) Restrict every teacher to three declarative sentences per class and fifteen interrogatives. Every sentence above this limit would be subject to a twenty-five cent fine. The students can do the counting and the collecting.

(6) Forbid any professor from asking a question to which he already knows the answer. This would insure that the professor learns something as well as the student.

(7) Abolish all tests and grades. This would destroy the professor's chief weapons of coercion, and would eliminate two obstacles to the students learning.

(8) Let students work through a level of achievement. If a student can advance through Speech 101 in five weeks let him do so. If it takes him a year that is his business. Make education an achievement, not a reward for sitting through a prescribed number of classroom hours and emerging victorious.

(9) Classify all professors according to their ability and make the lists public. There would be a smart group (the eagles), an average group (the bluebirds), and a dumb

group (the sparrows). The I.Q.s and reading scores of all professors should also be published as well as those who are "advantaged" and "disadvantaged."

(10) Require all instructors to take a test prepared by the students on the basis of what the students know. Only if a professor passes such a test should he be allowed to teach.

(11) Make every class an elective and withhold a teacher's paycheck if students show no interest in attending his classes. Check no absences. This proposal would place the college teacher on a level with other professional people. No one forces you to go to your doctor, your dentist or your lawyer; you go because you need to, and because you feel he can help you.

(12) Eliminate the English Proficiency and the Comprehensive Exam. If a student has no comprehension by the time he is a senior nothing can help him, not even God. If a student has taken twelve hours of English and still cannot write, it may be the fault of someone else.

(13) Require that all graffiti from whatever area of the college be collected, printed on a large banner and hung across the front of Murrah Hall, then we would all know what the students actually think.

(14) Organize a student demonstration and march on the National Educational Testing Service in Princeton, New Jersey and burn it to the ground. I will lead the march and light the fire.

In every speech, in every idea, in every proposal, there is a degree of truth. You may determine that percentage in this speech, but if we must oversimplify the question I will take the unequivocal position that "requirements are a deterrent to education." Peace!

Finishing time. _____

Now go to (29) .

(29)   Answer the following questions without looking back at the article. You aren't expected to be able to answer all the questions correctly if you read faster than you normally do.

1.   The main idea of the author is that

[ ]   a.   education needs to make some changes.

[ ]   b.   educational requirements are a deterrent to education.

[ ]   c.   educational requirements are an aid to education.

2.   The author's attitude toward his subject is one of

[ ]   a.   seriousness.

[ ]   b.   humor.

[ ]   c.   unable to tell.

3.   The author's statement, "Most of them [textbooks] are boring, poorly written, and almost all of them assume that knowledge exists prior to, independent of, and altogether outside of the learner" is a statement of fact.

_____ (true/false)

4.   The author feels that tests and grades are obstacles to student learning. _____ (true/false)

5.   The statement, "The I.Q.s and reading scores of all professors should also be published as well as those who are 'advantaged' and 'disadvantaged'" is a humorous "dig" at schools where students are separated according to abilities.

_____ (true/false)

6.   The author is opposed to the not taking of attendance in college classes. _____ (true/false)

7.   The reader can infer from the statement, "Make education an achievement, not a reward for sitting through a prescribed number of classroom hours . . ." that the author believes little real education is presently taking place in colleges.

_____ (true/false)

8.   For what does the author feel a professor should be fined?

_____

9.   Is the author's idea that teachers from Humanities teach
     Chemistry and Math and teachers from the Sciences teach

     English a good one? _____ Why? _____

_____

10. The reader can infer from the article that the author is lit-
     erally serious about leading a demonstration and march on

     the National Educational Testing Service. _____
     (true/false)

Check your answers in (30) .

---

1.   The best answer is b. You may have selected a, but it is
     more general than b. Read the last paragraph. It certainly
     is not c.

2.   This is a tricky question in some respects. The author is
     serious about educational changes, but his attitude and tone
     of the article is one of humor, answer b. His proposals,
     while based on what he sees as serious flaws in educational
     requirements, are a blend of humorous seriousness.

3.   False. While you (and I) may agree with it, the statement
     is one of opinion. There are no facts to prove what he says
     is true. They do seem that way at times, however. Proving
     the truth of that statement would be a good research project
     for you.

4.   True. See paragraph 7.

5.   True. Many schools group their classes according to IQ
     and refer to those with high scores as "advantaged" and
     those with low scores as "disadvantaged." The author
     throws the idea and the terms back at the teachers.

6.   False. This question is deliberately worded to cause you
     problems and force you to read carefully. The author is
     opposed to taking attendance. The word not makes the
     statement false.

7.   True. He is inferring that education is not really an
     achievement.

(continued)

8. Talking too much, specifically making more than three declarative and fifteen interrogative sentences in a class period. See paragraph 5.

9. Answers will vary and you'll have to be the judge of your correctness. Would you want an English instructor teaching you Chemistry? Will a professor interested in Philosophy do a good job of teaching you Algebra? Talk this over with some of your friends.

10. False. It is part of his humor in calling attention to facets of education with which he disagrees.

Go to ㉛ .

㉛ Count the number of correct responses you made on the comprehension check and multiply the number correct by 10 to get your percentage score.

Comprehension Score. _____

Subtract your starting time from your finishing time to see how many minutes and seconds it took you to read the article. Use the spaces below.

Finishing time. _____

Starting time. _____

Total reading time. _____

Use the chart below to determine the number of words per minute you read. Use the number of minutes and seconds listed which comes closest to your time and circle your WPM.

Time	WPM	Time	WPM
1:00	700	3:30	200
1:30	467	4:00	175
2:00	350	4:30	156
2:30	280	5:00	140
3:00	233	5:30	127

Record your WPM and comprehension score for Selection 4 in the chart on page 115. Then go to ㉜ .

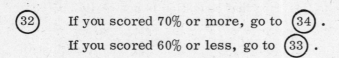

㉜ If you scored 70% or more, go to ㉞ .

If you scored 60% or less, go to �33 .

(33)   Sometimes readers understand much more than a comprehension quiz reveals; they just misread the questions. Sometimes the questions themselves are ambiguous, that is, capable of having more than one meaning. The most important question, if you read rapidly, is question 1. It calls for recognition of the main idea. If you got that one you're ahead of the game.

Take another look at the questions you missed and determine why you missed the ones you did. Then, in the listing below, check the appropriate reason or reasons for your differences in answers. Look at the frame indicated, and then come back here.

☐   read too fast to understand (see (34))

☐   misread the paragraph the point was in (see (35))

☐   misread the question (see (35))

☐   didn't understand the question(s) (see (36))

☐   don't agree with the answers (see (37))

☐   other: _____ (see (37))

Is there any pattern to your comprehension discrepancies? If you can see what you are doing wrong, try to avoid doing it on the next timed reading selections. If you can't, then you might consider enrolling in a reading course. Or, if you are already in a reading course, ask your instructor for some further diagnosis.

When you have reexamined your errors, take a break. Come back to (38) tomorrow when you're fresh and perky.

---

(34)   At first you were told not to worry if your comprehension scores drop when you try to read faster. It still may not be time to worry. However, if your rate is under 350 WPM with low comprehension, forget rate and develop your comprehension skills as directed in Chapter 1. If your rate is about 400 WPM or more with low comprehension, try slowing down just a bit, but not as slowly as you normally read.

Return to (33) .

---

(35)   Misreading a paragraph that contains a main point or a comprehension question is common when you are developing speed of comprehension. The fact that you know you misread the paragraph or the question is a good sign that you are aware of your problem.

(continued)

Keep analyzing your errors. By doing so, you are teaching yourself what to avoid in future drills by alerting your mind to pay closer attention to certain key words or phrases.

Return to (33) .

---

(36)   If you didn't understand the question or questions, then you can't really say you didn't know the answers. If the questions are not worded in a way you can answer them, then your comprehension score is not accurate. You may know the answer if the question were worded differently. You might need help in reading questions. See Carman and Adams' Study Skills: A Student's Guide for Survival. It has a good section on taking tests.

Return to (33) .

---

(37)   Can't help you too much here. This is not to say you're wrong; it's just that we can't get together and discuss your disagreements or other problems. The answer keys try to explain certain positions and reasoning, but you could still be correct. If you can back up your answers with actual statements from the article, give yourself credit for those answers.

Return to (33) .

---

(38)   Timed Reading Selection 5

Don't start this drill unless you have a watch or clock.

Time yourself while you read the following selection, "Canyon de Chelly National Monument."

Your purpose:

(1) Read as rapidly as you can, looking for the main idea.

(2) Be prepared to write a brief comment on the contents, but don't let this change of comprehension check slow you down.

(3) Don't vocalize.

(4) Don't regress.

(5) Don't let your mind wander.

Check your watch or clock and write down your starting time when you begin reading. Start exactly on the minute.

Starting time. _____

Begin reading.

CANYON DE CHELLY NATIONAL MONUMENT / ARIZONA

(1) These awesome canyons sheltered prehistoric Pueblo Indians for 1,000 years and served as an ancestral stronghold of the Navajo Indians. With its beautiful, steep-walled canyons and many ruins of prehistoric Indian dwellings nestled below towering cliffs or perched on high ledges, this monument typifies the colorful Southwestern Indian country. Adding to this atmosphere are the present-day Navajo Indian homes that are scattered along the canyon floors.

The Canyons

(2) The name De Chelly is a Spanish corruption of the Navajo word "Tsegi," which means roughly "rock canyon." The Spanish pronunciation "day shay-yee" has gradually changed through English usage, and the name is now pronounced "d'SHAY."

(3) The Spanish name of the chief tributary of Canyon de Chelly, Canyon del Muerto, means "Canyon of the Dead." It received its name in 1882, when a Smithsonian Institution expedition under James Stevenson found the remains of prehistoric Indian burials in this canyon.

(4) The Rio de Chelly rises near the Chuska Mountains close to the Arizona-New Mexico line and winds a tortuous course westward emptying into the Chinle Wash just west of the monument. Except for the last few miles, the Rio de Chelly and its tributaries are enclosed by vertical-walled canyons which

(continued)

range in depth from about 1,000 feet to only 30 feet at the mouth of Canyon de Chelly proper.

(5) The streams of this region flow during the rainy seasons and during the spring runoff of mountain snows; at other times they are dry. Sandstones, chiefly the De Chelly formation of Permian age, laid down more than 200 million years ago, compose the canyon walls. The reddish hue of the cliffs varies in intensity with the time of day.

Indian History

(6) In the canyons are ruins of several hundred prehistoric Indian villages, most of them built between A.D. 350 and 1300. The earliest known Indian occupants constructed individual, circular pithouses, so called because the lower parts of the dwellings were pits dug into the ground. Their chief weapon was a spear-throwing device, now called an atlatl. Not until later did they use the bow and arrow. They grew crops of maize and squash and made excellent baskets, sandals, and other woven articles; but they did not make pottery. Because of their fine basketry, these earliest Indians are commonly referred to as Basketmakers.

(7) In later centuries, the Basketmakers adopted many new ideas which were introduced into this area, such as the making of pottery, the bow and arrow, and bean cultivation. The style of their houses gradually changed through the years until finally they were no longer living in pithouses but were building rectangular houses of stone masonry above the ground which were connected together in compact villages. These changes basically altered Basketmaker life; and, because of the new "apartment house" style of their homes, the canyon dwellers after 700 are called Pueblos. Pueblo is the Spanish word for village, and it refers to the compact village life of these later people. Most of the large cliff houses in these canyons were built between 1100 and 1300, in the Pueblo period.

(8) During the 1200's, a prolonged drought parched what is now the Four Corners region of Arizona, Utah, Colorado, and New Mexico. About 1300, the drought, and perhaps other causes, forced the people of Canyon de Chelly and other nearby Pueblo centers to abandon their homes and scatter to other parts of the Southwest. Some of the present-day Pueblo Indians of Arizona and New Mexico are descendants of these pre-Columbian people. The canyons continued to be occupied sporadically by the early Hopi Indians of Arizona, also related to these Pueblo people. The Hopi were probably here only during the times when they were growing and harvesting crops.

(9) About 1700 the Navajo Indians, who were then concentrated in northern New Mexico, began to occupy Canyon de Chelly. An aggressive people related culturally and linguistically to the various Apache Indians in the Southwest, they raided for a century and a half the Pueblo Indian villages and Spanish settlements along the Rio Grande Valley. These attacks inspired the successive governments of New Mexico (Spanish, Mexican, and American) to make reprisals, and Canyon de Chelly became one of the chief Navajo strongholds.

(10) In 1805 a Spanish punitive expedition under Lt. Antonio Narbona, who later became governor of the Province of New Mexico, fought an all-day battle with a band of Navajos fortified in a rock shelter in Canyon del Muerto. Narbona's official report to the Governor stated that 115 Navajos were killed, including 90 warriors. Because of this, the rock shelter is called Massacre Cave.

(11) Navajo raids continued into the American period. A military campaign was begun and in 1864 a detachment of United States cavalry under Kit Carson engaged the Navajos in Canyon de Chelly. The raiding was brought to an end by the removal of more than 8,000 Navajos to new lands in eastern New Mexico.

(continued)

This first reservation experiment failed,
and after 4 years the Navajos were permitted
to return to their homeland.

(12) Today, many Navajos are salaried
employees. They still farm in a limited way,
but sheep herding, which they acquired from
the Spaniards in the 1700's, is declining
among them. Their distinctive circular
houses of logs and poles are called hogans.

Record your finishing time. _____

Go to (39) .

(39)   Previous exercises provided questions for you to answer as a
means of checking your comprehension. This time, without referring to the article, write a brief statement in the space below which
tells what the material you just read is about. Include what you
think is the main idea and at least nine other points you remember
reading about Canyon de Chelly National Monument.

Now go to (40) .

(40)   There is no answer key per se, but here is how you can check your summary. Look over what you wrote and give yourself 1 point if you said the main idea of the article was to give a history of Canyon de Chelly. Then for every one of the nine other statements you made in your summary, give yourself another point if you can locate the number of the paragraph in which what you wrote can be found. For instance, suppose you said that one of the points mentioned in the article was that the name Canyon de Chelly is a Spanish corruption of the Navajo word "Tsegi." Checking back by scanning the article, you find that this information is given in paragraph 2. Give yourself a point for that.

If you stated the main idea (1 point) and listed nine other items mentioned in the article, no matter how minor, then you have a total possibility of 10 points. Multiply the number of points you earned by 10 to obtain your percentage comprehension score. If you missed the main idea or did not remember nine points or ideas, then count off 1 point for each one you didn't get.

Comprehension Score. _____

Subtract your starting time from your finishing time.

Finishing time. _____

Starting time. _____

Total reading time. _____

Use the chart below to determine your reading rate (WPM). Circle the WPM corresponding to the number of minutes and seconds which comes closest to your reading time.

Time	WPM	Time	WPM
1:00	830	4:00	208
1:30	554	4:30	184
2:00	415	5:00	166
2:30	332	5:30	151
3:00	276	6:00	138
3:30	237	6:30	127

Record your comprehension score and WPM for Selection 5 in the chart on page 115. Then go to (41) .

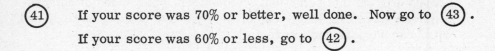

(41)   If your score was 70% or better, well done. Now go to (43) .
If your score was 60% or less, go to (42) .

Writing about what you read may seem more difficult than answering questions. However, some reading experts feel that writing a statement or summary about what is read is a better check of comprehension because there are no recall clues provided by some questions. Thus, the reader is forced to put what he read into his own words. Actually, this is a good test of how well you digested what you read.

Listing nine items should not have been difficult. Here are just a few examples.

1. Canyon de Chelly National Monument is in Arizona.
2. Prehistoric Pueblo Indians lived there for 1,000 years.
3. Present-day Navajos live in the area.
4. Indian homes are scattered along the canyon floor.
5. The name "de Chelly" is now pronounced "d'shay."
6. The name is derived from an Indian word meaning "rock canyon."
7. James Stevenson found the Canyon del Muerto in 1882.
8. Canyon de Chelly is near the Chuska Mountains.
9. The canyon walls are steep.

These nine points were all taken from the first four paragraphs. Many more could be taken from the rest of the article.

Go to 43 .

  <u>Timed</u> <u>Reading</u> <u>Selection</u> <u>6</u>

Don't begin this exercise unless you have your trusty timepiece.

The article you are about to read is longer than the previous timed reading selections and may seem more difficult than the others. The main difference is that the contents deal more with ideas than facts. By now, you may have realized that the selections have been progressively more demanding of you as a reader because of the concepts, vocabulary level, and style. This has been deliberate, and through that progression you have had an opportunity to practice with a variety of reading materials, just as you must do in the everyday "real" world of reading. This is mentioned so that you won't feel you are getting worse if your rate or comprehension scores drop on this selection. Remember, your speed of comprehension varies with length and difficulty of the reading matter, and with your purpose and interest.

Don't, however, let these comments be an excuse for you to slow down your rate.

Time yourself while you read the following article, "Critical Reading—As If There's Any Other Kind."

Your purpose:

(1) Read as fast as you can and still understand the main idea.

(2) Be prepared to write a short statement about what you read as well as answer some questions.

(3) Make mental notes of points you feel should be used in your statement to support what you think is the main idea.

(4) Look for the author's definition of a critical reader.

(5) Remember: don't vocalize; don't regress; don't let your mind wander.

Check your watch or clock and write down your starting time when you begin reading. Start exactly on the minute.

Starting time. _____

Begin reading.

CRITICAL READING—AS IF THERE'S ANY OTHER KIND

by Brother William J. Quaintance

(1) A number of authorities divide the act of reading into vocabulary or word recognition, comprehension, and interpretation or critical reading. The distinction between the latter two elements seems to arise from the notion that comprehension refers to understanding what the author has said, whereas interpretation consists in the evaluation of this information. Though it might be useful for academic purposes to make such a distinction, it becomes difficult and dangerous to attempt such a distinction in the reading situation itself. No one would advocate criticizing a work if the work has not been read. It is equally ludicrous to assume that anyone should ever say, "read this, but don't criticize it."

(continued)

(2) A clarification of "criticism" might be in order at this point. How often has the critic been compared to the reactionary or the obstructionist. How often have you prefaced a statement with, "I don't want to be critical, but . . .," or invoked the shibboleth of "constructive criticism," implying that criticism can be dangerous at times. To criticize means simply to evaluate, to assess, to state what is good and to state what is not good. A critic is neither an optimist nor a pessimist; he is merely an observer recording his findings.

(3) In one sense, it would be pleasant if criticism were unnecessary. Much mental effort would be spared if it could be guaranteed that a fact in print is a fact infallible. As a matter of fact, if the reader did not at times suspend his critical faculties somewhat and assume the validity of what he reads, his life would be chaotic. There is also efficiency in being able to go to a specific, reliable source for information. But there can be danger as well. When a person depends entirely on book learning to extend or to fortify his knowledge, he needs to read widely or he may eventually read only those sources which bolster his preconceived ideas.

(4) There is nothing more secure than ignorance, and nothing more exasperating at times than the insecurity of knowing just enough to realize one's limitations. How glibly the regular in the corner bar solves all the problems of the world, problems which those in authority have great difficulty even defining. The college undergraduate soon knows all the answers, then in graduate school he learns some of the questions. A teacher is encouraged when her students have learned enough to verbalize a coherent question. If criticism is done properly, the critic will never be secure in the sense of being rigidly bound to a past commitment. He will be sufficiently secure in his present scale of values, however, to be able to tolerate the suspension

of judgment which precedes the acceptance or
rejection of new data. The insecurity within
the individual is caused by the limitations of
his present information. It does not arise
from undue commitment in the past, nor lack
of confidence in the future.

(5) The critical reader knows that his
present fund of information is reliable, because he subjects it to constant evaluation.
He also knows the relative value of each item
in his hierarchy of values. He is aware of
which concepts are the fixed stars and con-
stellations that guide his life, which concepts
are dependent satellites, and which are but
meteors of brief intensity.

(6) Criticism may be concerned with the
author (writer or speaker), the material
(written or spoken), or the receiver (listener
or reader). The material itself may be description, explicit or inferred comment, or
most often a combination of the two. In order
to determine the proportions of subjectivity
and objectivity, the reader must know the
contents of the material and the purpose for
which it was written, which leads to a consideration of the author. Is he merely trying
to convey information "for what it's worth"
without any benefit to himself? Hardly, because his reputation as an authority and the
incomes of himself and his publisher may depend on the number of people who accept his
presentation. And if the author proposes to
convince as well as inform, he may sacrifice
objectivity for chiaroscuro. Some areas of
his picture may be brightened, others ob-
scured, by downright lies or some of the ques-
tionable techniques of propaganda. And even
if his own motives are above reproach, the
author may have been the victim of such devices. Moreover, an idea may be right for
the wrong reason ("don't steal if the cops are
around"), or wrong even if one of its allegedly
supporting facts happens to be true (discrim-
ination is wrong, even if proportionately more
crimes are commited by Negroes). Forgeries,

(continued)

typographical errors, and the like can also affect the validity of the material.

(7) Since neither the author nor the material can be counted on to be consistently free from error, the reader is the person who must determine truth as best he can. He stops asking, "when do I read critically?" because he sees that he must do so whenever he desires accurate information.

(8) What constitutes a critical reader? First, a critical reader must be biased. Not prejudiced, which he would be if he has formed conclusions without, or in spite of, supporting evidence; but biased, when he has come to a sincere conclusion on the basis of his background of experience with the subject in question. In other words, he must have a stand on the subject under investigation. If he has no stand—we use the term "open mind," though "empty mind" would sometimes be more appropriate—he may accept the first presentation which reaches him, because he lacks sufficient background to dispute the point. At best, he can delay final acceptance of the information pending direct experience or further consultation with other sources.

(9) As was pointed out above, there is no intrinsic evil in accepting an authority's word for something. Difficulty arises when the reader forgets that verification must always be possible and permissible. Neither is there any problem in having the reader defer his acceptance of a "fact" until he has gathered additional data. The basic premise of criticism is that accurate data need not fear criticism. If a fact is acceptable at all it should remain acceptable when all of the pertinent data are available. Conversely, if acceptance of an idea is contingent on the suppression or distortion of certain factors in its makeup, there is something wrong with it. If a concept cannot tolerate criticism, it should not survive at all.

(10) The author's purpose is the factor which determines the extent of his elaboration. He can describe how to drive a car without discussing the mechanics of internal combustion, and explain the process of reproduction without accounting for the chemical structure of amniotic fluid. Nevertheless, the reader should have available all of the detail he needs to understand the author's ideas. If the reader is aware that certain data are not supplied, he should be able to determine whether this omission will interfere with the purpose for which he is reading.

(11) The second characteristic of a critical reader is his willingness to modify a present viewpoint. If a reader is certain that he is right, he will not even consider a change. If he is in error, he is usually unaware of it. Only a critical reader avails himself of opportunities to verify and possibly improve his present fund of information. The person who is always right may not care about the views of someone else. If these other views match his own, his ego is bolstered, but he will explain away or ignore any view that conflicts with his own, because if he were to learn that something else is correct his life would be filled with unbearable contradictions. To avoid such contradictions he must become (pardon the etymological pun) hypocritical.

(12) But what happens when he accepts the possibility that he does not have all the answers, and that some of his answers may be incorrect? For one thing, the critical reader will compare his ideas with those of someone else. If the other source is correct, the critical reader has expanded his knowledge; if he is correct and the source is in error, he has strengthened his own position and probably equipped himself to deal with the error he has encountered. Either way he benefits. Arthur Koestler, in "The Eureka Process," uses the term "bisociation" to describe how brilliant insights and solutions to

(continued)

problems have been achieved when savants were willing to leave a preconceived frame of reference to relate otherwise ordinary concepts in original and unconventional ways.

(13)   The third characteristic of a critical reader is that he be willing to involve himself in the consequences of a fact, once he accepts it. In some instances this involves nothing more than going along with the thought of the majority; at other times it may cost him his life and reputation if reading leads him to a personal commitment to action.

(14)   No one bothers to dispute the point that the <u>Aedes</u> <u>aegypti</u> mosquito is instrumental in transmitting yellow fever, nor does any one fear being known as favoring the elimination of this insect. The average reader has had no direct experience with yellow fever and knows it only from history, geography, or medicine. He has accepted all of this information because (1) several independent sources agreed on this fact, sources which were usually correct in other items or at other times when he consulted them; (2) these sources had no motive for deceiving him; (3) it makes little difference to him what the cause of yellow fever is, because in these times it has no direct bearing on his life.

(15)   Now, instead of mosquitoes and yellow fever, use the example of cigarettes and lung cancer. You probably have become critical because you have a bias on this topic. Your commitment on this question may have a number of consequences regarding your personal smoking habits, or whether you should allow others to smoke if you are in a position to control their behavior, whether you should watch a television show sponsored by a tobacco concern, or read a magazine which carries tobacco advertising. Your reaction to the question will be affected by whether you run a store which sells tobacco products, live in a state where tobacco is an important crop, or have had a relative who died of lung cancer. You could delay your decision,

"waiting for more information on the subject,"
but even this will force you to act provision-
ally on one side or the other. You could also
deny the evidence. After all, "it's only sta-
tistical."

(16) In a penetrating essay, "The Critical
Reader," Edgar Dale distinguishes between
reading the lines, reading between the lines,
and reading beyond the lines. "Reading can
be taught as training," observes Dale, "with
fixed limits and predictable responses. Genuine educational experiences, however, have
no ceiling, no fixed boundaries, no terminal
points." It is probably this factor of involvement, more than the others, which discour-
ages genuine critical reading and generates
so much of the apathy that exists in schools
and communities. Children begin life with a
zest for knowledge and curiosity about everything, but somewhere along the way they
surrender this inquisitive spirit for the much
less disturbing routine of conformity. Perhaps they discovered unpleasantly that a fact
which enlightens some people will "burn up"
others. They discover that critical people
tend to annoy those who prefer the security
of convention to the risks and rewards of
scholarship. As the Talmud so wisely says,
"He who would tell the truth must have one
foot in the stirrup." The whole idea of personal involvement is based on acting in conformity with convictions. The heroes of
history are those who had such strong convictions that they were willing to make any
sacrifice to preserve them.

Record your finishing time here. _____

Go to (44) .

1. In the space below write a brief statement or summary of the author's definition of a critical reader.

2. What does the author mean by the following statements?

    a. "When a person depends entirely on book learning to extend or to fortify his knowledge, he needs to read widely or he may eventually read only those sources which bolster his preconceived ideas."

    _____

    _____

    b. "The critical reader knows that his present fund of information is reliable, because he subjects it to constant evaluation."

    _____

    _____

    c. "Since neither the author nor the material can be counted on to be correct or to be consistently free from error, the reader is the person who must determine truth as best he can."

    _____

    _____

    d. "Children begin life with a zest for knowledge and curiosity about everything, but somewhere along the way they surrender this inquisitive spirit for the much less disturbing routine of conformity."

    _____

    _____

Now go to .

(45)   Answers will vary in wording, but there should be similarities in content or explanation with the answers that follow. Compare yours with them.

1.   According to the author, a critical reader must first be biased or have an opinion about the subject (see paragraph 8). Secondly, he must be willing to change his viewpoint about a topic (see paragraph 11). Next, he must be willing to involve himself in the results of what he accepts (see paragraph 13). (<u>Note:</u> These are the three basic points made in defining a critical reader. If your summary includes others, scan the article for the three paragraphs listed in the sample answer above to see if your comments are included in any of these three major sections of the essay. While the author rambles a bit, he does offer these three major divisions in his essay. Yet, because he does ramble, it is possible you remembered minor points he mentions under the major points. It would be easy to do in this article.)

2.   a. The author means that book learning is limited, and when it is a reader's only source of information, he'd better read a lot and from many sources, not just those which support his own views.

b. A critical reader constantly criticizes and evaluates what he reads before accepting it as reliable.

c. A critical reader knows that authors are human and biased, thus what appears in print is not free from errors and cannot always be relied upon as "truth" or "fact."

d. Somewhere along the line of life, we lose our critical curiosity and begin to accept what we hear or read as fact, rather than being as curious and investigative as we were when children.

These are just sample answers and subject to error, too. However, if you don't agree with these or if you are in doubt about your answers, scan the article for the place where the author's statements occur. See how they are used in context. Then judge your answers for accuracy. According to the author of the article you just read, you're not a critical reader if you accept the sample answers; you'll check for yourself. So apply what you just read!

Give yourself 20 points for each correct answer, for a possible total of 100 points. If you only answered part of a question correctly, then give yourself less than 20 points for it, based on your judgment of what you think you deserve. Be fair to yourself.

Comprehension Score. _____

(continued)

Subtract your starting time from your finishing time.

Finishing time. _____

Starting time. _____

Total reading time. _____

Use the table below to determine your reading rate. Circle the WPM corresponding to the minutes and seconds closest to your actual reading time.

Time	WPM	Time	WPM
1:00	2200	6:00	350
2:00	1050	6:30	323
2:30	975	7:00	300
3:00	700	7:30	280
3:30	648	8:00	262
4:00	526	8:30	247
4:30	470	9:00	233
5:00	420	9:30	221
5:30	382	10:00	210

Record your comprehension score and WPM for Selection 6 on page 115. Then take a break. Tomorrow, start with (46).

---

(46)   Timed Reading Selection 7

Don't start reading this selection unless you have a watch or clock.

Time yourself while you read the following article, "The Ambiguous American." (Ambiguous means unclear or capable of being understood in more ways than one.)

Your purpose:

(1) Read to understand what the author means by "The Ambiguous American."

(2) Read to remember the six characteristics of the American which he calls "common denominators" or characteristics shared by most Americans.

(3) Read without vocalizing, regressing, or letting your mind wander.

Starting time. _____

Begin reading.

THE AMBIGUOUS AMERICAN
(Part One)

by Henry Steele Commager

(1) Few Old World countries have been preoccupied with the search for national identity; because they are the products of history, with their own language, culture and traditions, they can take their character for granted. Americans have never been able to take themselves for granted in this comfortable fashion. They have been conscious—perhaps they are still conscious—that they were a new nation, and one made out of the most miscellaneous materials, their language, their laws, their culture inherited from the Old World.

(2) At the same time they have, from the beginning, been sure that their nation did have a character of its own, a special character and a special destiny. Franklin noted distinctly "American traits" even before independence, and most of the Founding Fathers were determined that the new nation should differ profoundly from the nations of the Old World. From St. John Crevecoeur and Condorcet to Tocqueville and Grattan, from Bryce and Munsterberg to Brogan and Myrdal, foreign observers drew confidently the lineaments of "that new man, the American."

(3) We have then impressive authority for asserting that there are indeed American traits. To enumerate such traits does not in any way imply that they are unique to the Americans; most Western peoples, after all, share a common character. Nor does it imply that all Americans reveal these traits. Americans are a heterogeneous and individualistic people. And it would certainly be an error to suppose that such traits as we may assign to the American are in any sense inherent. They are,

(continued)

rather, the product of environment and experience; both of these have changed and continue to change.

(4) Let us see if we can distinguish some common denominators in the American character.

(5) 1. Perhaps the most common, and the most pervasive, is carelessness. The American is careless in his manners, his dress and his address; he is careless about his house and his garden; careless in social relationships, shuffling off old and taking on new with utmost casualness; careless about observing laws, rules and regulations; careless about his food and his drink, and impatient with ceremony; careless about money.

(6) He tends to be careless about larger things as well: his social relationships, his educational system and his politics. He has a long tradition of carelessness toward nature. He used up the soil, burned down the forests, polluted the streams, killed off the buffalo and the pigeons; he turns nature into a desert and his cities into junkyards.

(7) 2. The American is, on the whole, openhanded, generous and hospitable. No other people pours so much money into churches, schools, hospitals and other charities; no other has given so freely to help less fortunate people around the globe. While it is true that a system of tax exemptions makes it easy for Americans to be generous, it is suggestive that American tax laws are designed to encourage giving. The great philanthropic foundation is a distinctly American institution, almost an American invention.

(8) For two centuries visitors from the Old World have paid tribute to American hospitality; the American—as Denis Brogan has observed—was the first to make the term "stranger" a word of welcome. Along with material generosity went magnanimity. It is not without significance that America achieved nationalism without recourse to national en-

mities; Americans did not nurse enmity toward
Britain in the 19th century, nor have they har-
bored enmity toward Germany or Japan in the
20th.

(9)   Though they have won most of their
wars, they have never imposed a vengeful
peace upon the vanquished.   Southerners fancy
that the North imposed a "Punic peace" upon
them in 1865, but the fact is that when the
war was over, no one lost his life because
of the rebellion, and Southerners were back
in Congress within a year after Appomattox.
Compare this with what happened to unsuc-
cessful rebels in Scotland, Ireland, France,
Italy, Spain, Cuba or Russia in modern times.

(10)   There are exceptions, to be sure.   We
were not generous toward the Indian in the 19th
century, or the Mexican.   Though our immi-
gration policy was on the whole hospitable, we
were something less than generous in our attitude toward the refugees from totalitarianism
in the nineteen-forties and fifties.

(11)   3.   Much of American generosity
springs from good fortune and abundance.
These account, too, for a third American
trait: self-indulgence.   The American dearly
loves comfort and is acquiring a taste for
luxury.   He pampers himself, his wife and
his children.   He rides instead of walking;
overheats his house, his office and even his
car; thinks himself entitled to frequent and
long vacations, to summers in the North Woods
and winters in Florida.   He spends enough on
tobacco, liquors and cosmetics to pay off the
national debt; drives his children to school
instead of letting them walk or ride bicycles;
marries young and takes for granted help from
his parents.

(12)   The Declaration of Independence included the pursuit of happiness as a natural
right, and the American is obsessed with this
pursuit.   He is sure that providence and nature mean him to be happy and he regards any

(continued)

interference with the attainment of happiness
as a violation of natural law. Advertisements
proclaim this more blatantly in America than
elsewhere. What is achieved by the cigarette,
the vacation in Florida, the electric mixer,
the new car, is happiness.

(13) 4. This expectation of happiness be-
speaks a strong strain of sentimentality and
even romanticism. The American is sentimental about many things: children, the little
red schoolhouse, the "old" South, nature, college, war and sports. Where else do men and
women rise and uncover as they solemnly intone
the Alma Mater at some athletic event; where
else, for that matter, do they have college
songs?

(14) American advertisements ooze senti-
ment; American movies and television purvey
it relentlessly—along with a good deal of quite
unsentimental sadism, to be sure. If novels
are not so sentimental as they were in the 19th
century, the stories that trickle through the
advertisements in women's magazines still are.

(15) 5. One of the more amiable of American traits is gregariousness. It is doubtless
a product of New World circumstances, of a
society that has been atomized and is anxious
to knit new ties of association to take the place
of the old; of a frontier environment where
men banded together to conquer nature and
isolation; to equalitarianism, which looked with
suspicion on anyone who held aloof from his
fellow men.

(16) Americans like to do things together
and take comfort in numbers. They are the
world's most enthusiastic joiners; they do not
want to read alone or walk alone, but join clubs
so they can do these things in common. They
do not prize privacy, but company, and they
submit cheerfully to continuous invasions of
privacy—music blaring at them in train and
plane, commercials shouting at them over
radio and television, the badges worn so con-
spicuously at every convention.

(17) The American tends to distrust the man who lives to himself, who prefers reading to conversation on a bus or a plane, who does not join fraternities or clubs and who hesitates to use first names.

(18) 6. On one American trait almost all European critics are agreed: materialism. Is the American in fact more materialistic than his European cousins? Perhaps he is merely more honest. He is intensely conscious of the material world in which he lives, the world of natural abundance, the world of industry and business. He is conscious, too, of size and space. Almost two centuries ago Crevecoeur observed that the overwhelming impact of size and environment, at once enlarged and elevated the ideas of the American; a hundred miles, he said, were now what a mile had been before.

(19) The United States was, at birth, the largest of Western nations, and for over a century the American imagination was fired by the prospect of "land enough for our descendants to the thousandth and thousandth generation," by vast mountain ranges, limitless prairies, lakes as large as oceans. Nor should it be forgotten that, if the "land was ours before we were the land's," the process of becoming American was in part one of identification with the natural environment.

(20) History, too, emphasized material considerations; if the new nation was to preserve its independence in a hostile world and realize its democratic potential, it had to grow and grow fast.

(21) No wonder the American has always been fascinated by size and figures. No wonder he takes pride in the largest lakes, the tallest trees, the most rapidly growing cities. It is fair to add that fascination with material growth has not in fact made the American more materialistic than the Frenchman or German. It is reassuring to note that American power

(continued)

and wealth have commonly been made available to other peoples for benevolent purposes.

Record your finishing time here. _____

Now go to ⟨47⟩ .

⟨47⟩ Answer the following questions without looking back at the article.

1. The main idea of the article is that

☐ a. Americans have no character.

☐ b. the characteristics of Americans are linked with
the Old World.

☐ c. there are recognizable American traits.

2. The author's attitude toward his subject is

☐ a. serious.

☐ b. humorous.

☐ c. indifferent.

3. According to the author, the American has always been

fascinated by size. _____ (true/false)

4. List the six characteristics of the American you were told
to look for. You may use your own wording.

_____

_____

_____

_____

_____

5. The reader can infer from the author's comments and attitude

that he is proud of Americans. _____ (true/false)

Check your answers in ⟨48⟩ .

1. c; see paragraph 3, first sentence. The author takes the first two paragraphs to set up his thesis or views about his subject. By paragraph 3 he is ready to begin stating his main idea. The rest of the essay supports his views in paragraph 3.

2. a; he is rather matter-of-fact and straightforward.

3. True; see the last paragraph. This is a test of recall and not important to understanding the article.

4. Your wording may differ, but the meanings should be similar: careless (see paragraph 5); generous or open-handed (see paragraph 7); self-indulgent (see paragraph 11); sentimental or romantic (see paragraph 13); gregarious or liking people (see paragraph 15); materialistic (see paragraph 18). Since you were told to look for these six points, that should have been your purpose. The author also numbered them for you so you would recognize each new point he made.

5. True; notice that even though he shows some faults, he generally praises the American, especially for his generousness. Notice, too, the last sentence ends the essay on a note of praise.

Now go to (49) .

---

(49)   Count the number of correct answers. Each item in question 4 counts as 1 point. In other words, if you knew all six answers in question 4, you receive 6 points for that question. If you missed one of the items you receive 5 points, and so on. There is a total of 10 points possible. Multiply your correct answers by 10%.

Comprehension Score. _____

If your score was 70% or more, nice going. Go to (51) .

If your score was 60% or less, go to (50) .

---

(50)   Chances are that you missed most of your points in answering question 4. It required you to recall without clues what you read. Remember that before you began reading the article you were told there were six characteristics and your purpose was to read to see what they were. Foremost in your mind, then, should have been to remember those six points. The author even numbered them for you so that they were easy to identify.

(continued)

Take another look at the questions you missed and reread the parts of the article where the correct answer appears. Notice such things as paragraphs 5 and 6 and how often the author uses the word "careless," one of the six traits. Notice, too, that in practically every paragraph which names one of the six traits that the trait appears in the first sentence of the paragraph and that the remaining sentences merely give support, examples, or clarify what the author means.

When you have finished analyzing your errors, go to (51) .

(51)   Subtract your starting time from your finishing time to determine your total reading time.

        Finishing time.   _____

        Starting time.   _____

        Total reading time.   _____

Use the table below to figure your WPM. Use the number of minutes and seconds closest to your reading time and circle your rate.

Time	WPM	Time	WPM
1:00	1400	5:00	280
1:30	933	5:30	245
2:00	700	6:00	233
2:30	560	6:30	215
3:00	467	7:00	200
3:30	400	7:30	186
4:00	350	8:00	175
4:30	311	8:30	165

Record your comprehension score and WPM for Selection 7 in the chart on page 115. Then come back here.

If your WPM was 245 or more, go to (53) .

If your WPM was 233 or less, go to (52) .

(52)   This article was not a particularly easy one to read rapidly. In fact, it is more difficult than any of the others because of the concepts and vocabulary used. Don't feel too badly if your rate was slow, provided you did well on the comprehension quiz. Remember that speed itself is not too important. Comprehension is. If you need to read slowly to understand better, then do it. You should

not get the impression that because all the drills in the chapter are timed that speed is the important thing.   They are provided for development of comprehension as well as speed.

It's not easy to change a lifetime reading habit; it takes lots of time and patience and practice.   By now you know the techniques and means for changing those habits which may be keeping you from achieving the reading goals you have set for yourself.   Just keep on practicing until you feel you have reached your maximum potential.

It may be that you have already reached your top level in speed of comprehension, but chances are that continued practice of the methods described and shown to you will result in more of an increase than you feel now.   But, if you don't really need the speed, forget it and concentrate on developing comprehension.

Now go to (53) .

---

(53)   If the scores on the chart on page 115 have gone up in comprehension and/or WPM, you can visually see your growth.   However, the scores are not really an indication of what you have actually learned because they represent exercises you did to practice changing your reading habits.   Your scores could even have gone down, because the reading selections are increasingly difficult.   So in reality you might be reading better than you ever have because of what you learned from the exercises.   At any rate, you have started to do something about your speed of comprehension and it will be up to you to continue.

Remember, to develop speed of comprehension:

(1)   Practice reading at least twenty minutes daily, avoiding vocalization and regression habits.

(2)   Pace yourself to read faster than you normally do.

(3)   Read from a wide variety of materials.

(4)   Don't sacrifice speed for comprehension.

(5)   Continue to develop your vocabulary skills, using one of the methods described in Chapter 1.

If you have been averaging 250 WPM or less on the last three selections, you probably would benefit from doing the following practice exercise sets as part of your daily practice routine.

(continued)

If you have been averaging 300 WPM or more on the last three selections, you are reading a bit above the average high school graduate's rate. If you are satisfied with this, go on to the next or another chapter. If you want to continue to build speed of comprehension, go to the practice sets, which begin on the next page. This concludes the chapter on improving speed of comprehension.

PRACTICE EXERCISES FOR DEVELOPING
SPEED OF COMPREHENSION

The following exercises are not programmed; rather they are grouped into sets. It is best if you do only one set of exercises in each practice session. They are designed to help you speed up your perceptual ability and to overcome vocalization and regression tendencies. As other drills in this chapter, they should be timed.

Set I

Exercise 1

Directions: Below are two columns of phrases. Together, the phrases make no sense so do not attempt to read for comprehension. The object is to read down the two columns and to mark the phrase never before every time you see it in either column. Do not let your lips move. Place a pencil between your lips if you need to do so. You should finish in less than 20 seconds.

Begin timing.

not right now	in summary
never before	in essence
like this one	in demand
in all respect	never new
for the time	never before
never before	before today
in the summer	from the top
never ending	to forget it
write a summary	never before
light brown	now is time
never ending	for the truth
from a farm	never before
when it lives	over the bridge
before the end	my ten cents
never before	never before

Record your time. _____ (20 seconds is average)

The phrase never before appears seven times. Count the number of phrases you marked.

Exercise 2

Directions: Underline the phrase <u>garage</u> <u>mechanic</u> every time it appears in the group of phrases below. Do not regress. Keep your eyes moving from left to right without backtracking.

Begin timing.

greatly needed   not before now   garage
mechanic   from this moment   never before
garage mechanic   garage training   near my
heart   it is necessary   garbage disposal
beside the lake   reading fast   garage mechanic
mechanical doll   for the first   garage
mechanic   program guide

Record your time. _____ (15 seconds is average)

You should have marked <u>garage</u> <u>mechanic</u> four times. Check your markings. If you took more than 20 seconds you are probably regressing. Don't worry about mistakes. Practice moving your eyes correctly.

Exercise 3

Directions: Underline the phrase <u>greatly</u> <u>damaged</u> every time it appears in the group of phrases below. Do not let your eyes regress. Move them rapidly and don't stop to change any mistakes you make.

Begin timing.

greatly concerned   not before now   from
this moment   greatly damaged   beside the lake
group of words   garage mechanic   greatly
damaged   on Sundays only   near my heart
greatly damaged   some other time   count me
out   greatly damaged   try it again   book titles
it is necessary   tell me later

Record your time. _____ (15 seconds is average)

You should have marked <u>greatly</u> <u>damaged</u> four times. Check your markings. Mistakes in marking are less important than correct eye movements.

Exercise 4

Directions: Practice moving your eyes quickly from left to right. In the groups of words on the next page, when you see the word on the left by the number appearing somewhere on the same line, mark it quickly and go to the next line, doing the same thing with the next numbered word. Do not vocalize and do not regress. If you make a mistake, don't stop to change it. Keep moving along until you are finished with all ten lines.

Begin timing.

1. ambush   adventure alimony animal actual ambush
2. ballad   bullet ballot ballad bomb bumpy
3. clack   cluck clack click clod cloud
4. deduct   deduce depend devout deduct detour
5. fraud   frown freak fraud frank front
6. guide   guide guilty goon grind grump
7. humbug   hungry hump help humbug hovel
8. literal   lively literal little limp listed
9. lucid   lovely lively literal lucid lacks
10. wraith   wrapped wreath wrough wait wraith

Record your time. _____ (25 seconds is average)

Check each line to see if you marked the correct words.

Exercise 5

Directions: Practice skimming straight down a newspaper column of your choice. Time yourself three times on the same column, trying to outdo yourself each time.

Practice 1. _____ seconds

Practice 2. _____ seconds

Practice 3. _____ seconds

This ends Set I. Do not go on to Set II for at least 12 hours.

Set II

Exercise 1

Directions: Mark the key phrase happy days every time it appears in the columns below. Do not vocalize or regress.

Begin timing.

the measure was	happy days	would result
happy days	broken into	the attitude of
heavy container	scores more	widely known
justice itself	damaged heart	happy days
the same time	his attitude	has been seen
heart's broken	blindness is	never mind
happy days	right to burst	such a deal
another warning	happy days	hearts beat
it may not	contented heart	happy days
handle this	same as before	liquid fuel

Record your time. _____ (20 seconds is average)

The phrase happy days appears six times. Count the number of phrases you marked.

Exercise 2

Directions: Underline the phrase reading comprehension every time it appears in the group of phrases below. Do not vocalize or regress.

Begin timing.

The entire paragraph   never before   from
here to there   reading comprehension   near
the building   reading skills   poor comprehension
reading comprehension   guide the way   reading
concentration   reading comprehension   greatly
needed   swim for miles   buy it now   see the light
don't bother me   reading comprehension   several
more   is this the way   read and study   reading
skills

Record your time. _____ (15 seconds is average)

You should have marked reading comprehension four times. Check your markings.

Exercise 3

Directions: Underline the phrase don't regress each time it appears in the group of phrases below. Don't vocalize or regress.

Begin timing.

A popular pastime   during a longer   from
now on   don't regress   you can find   can be used
large and roomy   don't regress   too nice for it
rent is due   don't regress   three-day weekend
on my time   a number of them   don't regress
more than most   buried within   large and roomy
tell me more   some time this year   don't
regress   that's all for now

Record your time. _____ (15 seconds is average)

You should have marked don't regress five times. Check your markings.

Exercise 4

Directions: Practice moving your eyes quickly from left to right. When you see the word on the left by the number appearing somewhere on the same line, mark it quickly and go to the next line, doing the same thing with the next numbered word. Do not vocalize or regress. If you make a mistake, don't stop to change it. Keep moving along until you are finished with all ten lines.

Begin timing.

1. control   comrade capital create control curious
2. planned   plan planned prepare quote plotted
3. several   sincere speculate several special spots
4. possess   proud prepare quotation proceed possess
5. achieve   retrieve achievement mischief achieve attach
6. whose   whom which who whose whether
7. favorite   favor fatter fasten facet favorite
8. privilege   principle privilege practice positive play
9. using   useful using usual underhanded
10. response   repose replace rerun response replacement

Record your time. _____ (25 seconds is average)

Check each line to see if you marked the correct word.

Exercise 5

Directions: Practice skimming straight down a newspaper column of your choice. Time yourself three times on the same column, trying to outdo yourself each time.

Practice 1. _____ seconds

Practice 2. _____ seconds

Practice 3. _____ seconds

Compare your time with Exercise 5 in Set I.

This ends Set II. Do not go on to Set III for at least 12 hours.

Set III

Exercise 1

Directions: Mark the key phrase <u>possible</u> <u>reaction</u> every time it appears in the columns below. Do not vocalize or regress.

Begin timing.

rent a car	the latter type
share the cost	popular pastime
you and me	possible reaction
public service	between three
with my wife	your gear
possible reaction	more sedentary
from noon on	he's a wreck
public rooms	possible reaction
possible reaction	public utilities
in the center	for the day
more relaxing	a few large
possible reaction	in some areas
slowing down	pony express
with a room	etiquette demands
the whole one	possible reaction

Record your time. _____ (20 seconds is average)

The phrase <u>possible</u> <u>reaction</u> appears six times. Count the number of phrases you marked.

Exercise 2

Directions: Underline the phrase <u>synthetic</u> <u>fertilizers</u> each time it appears in the group of phrases below.

Begin timing.

Rental conditions   operating procedures
the wrong time   never on Saturdays   symphonic
music   large waterfalls   synthetic fertilizers
scheduled ahead   synthetic parts   sucrose in
large parts   aside from water   consider syn-
thetics   confident of gains   science first
symbols of gold   the above material   that's
all folks

Record your time. _____ (15 seconds is average)

You should have marked <u>synthetic</u> <u>fertilizers</u> once. Check your marking.

Exercise 3

Directions: Using your finger as a pacer, force your eyes to follow your finger as you read rapidly from left to right.

Begin timing.

> Houseboating has become a popular pastime in many parts of the country. The boats are large and roomy and they can be used during a longer period of the year than most other types of watercraft. Most houseboats cost from $10,000 to $15,000, but fortunately a number of rental operators have gone into business and you can rent one relatively inexpensively if you share the cost between three or four couples.

Record your time. _____ (15 seconds is average)

Without looking back, write a brief statement about what you read. Then reread the paragraph to check your answer.

Exercise 4

Directions: Using your finger as a pacer, force your eyes to follow your finger as you read rapidly from left to right.

Begin timing.

> Sugar cane is grown with the use of synthetic fertilizers and weed sprays. The fields are burned just previous to harvest. These are destructive agricultural practices; nothing truly good can come from soil so mistreated. I would, therefore, be uninterested in commercially grown sugar cane, either brown sugar or molasses.

Record your time. _____ (20 seconds is average)

Without looking back, write a brief statement about what you read. Then reread the paragraph to check your answer.

Exercise 5

Directions: Practice skimming straight down a newspaper column of your choice. Time yourself three times on the same column, trying to outdo yourself each time.

Practice 1. _____ seconds

Practice 2. _____ seconds

Practice 3. _____ seconds

Compare your time with Exercise 5 in Set II.

This concludes the practices for this chapter.

CHAPTER FOUR
Improving Study Reading

GOALS AND OBJECTIVES

General Goals: When you complete this chapter you will be able to:

(1) Apply a general approach to reading textbooks.

(2) Apply systematic procedures for more effective study reading.

(3) Have increased confidence when reading textbook assignments.

(4) Score higher on exams based on textbook assignments.

Specific Objectives: When you complete this chapter you will be able to:

(1) Recall the meaning of SQ3R.

(2) Adopt the SQ3R technique for study reading textbooks.

(3) Survey each chapter before reading it in detail.

(4) Formulate study-guide questions based on this survey before reading the chapter in detail.

(5) Use some systematic method of recitation to review the content of the chapter.

(6) Review the chapter after reading by referring to your notes and textbook markings.

(7) Apply what has been learned by using the tear-out sheets at the end of this chapter.

If you want to learn an effective approach to study reading so that you can get more from your study time, read on.

Check the following boxes which apply to you.

☐ 1.   You start reading an assignment by going to the first page of the assignment and beginning there.

☐ 2.   Your mind wanders to other things while you are reading.

☐ 3.   You don't pay much attention to footnotes, captions under pictures, or charts and graphs.

☐ 4.   You mark and underline your books as you read.

☐ 5.   You panic when you take a test.

☐ 6.   You spend hours studying with little to show for it.

If you checked four or more of these items, you're in the right place. If you didn't mark at least four items—well, read on for a while anyway and see if you can learn some tricks about study reading.

There it is, sitting on your desk in front of you—a $12.00 psychology textbook, heavy in weight and content. You're supposed to read the first chapter before your 8 o'clock class tomorrow, so you turn to Chapter One and start reading, right?

Wrong! That would be like taking a picture without focusing on your subject and correctly setting the lens opening. What you need is a plan of attack—a plan that helps you use your study-reading time wisely and that offers you long lasting results. Without that plan, the results of your study reading will be as fuzzy as a picture out of focus.

Although every student has his own approach to study reading, there are some general approaches which lead to good results. These generalities have been condensed into a very well known and usable formula: SQ3R. The term SQ3R is a mnemonic device (memory aid) designed to help you remember the five general steps for good study reading. <u>Learn these five steps in the following order</u>.

S   = Survey

Q   = Question

R^1 = Read

R^2 = Recite

R^3 = Review

There are many variations of this formula. But it is important that you remember each of the five steps and the proper sequence of each step. Once you learn in more detail what these steps are and how to use them, you can adapt them to fit your particular study needs. But before we get into a detailed description of the formula and how you should apply it, let's see how well you understand what you've read so far.

Which one of the following is correct?

Survey, Question, Read, Review, Recite [ ] Go to (1).

Survey, Question, Read, Recite, Repeat [ ] Go to (2).

Survey, Question, Read, Recite, Review [ ] Go to (3).

---

(1)   Nope. You probably weren't paying attention to the correct order of SQ3R, but it's important. Go back and look at the order of the formula again. Repeat it until you can recite the correct order. Then choose another answer.

---

(2)   Where did you get the idea that "Repeat" was one of the five steps? You are close but not close enough. Take another look at the formula as it was first presented. Say it to yourself until you have it. Then try another answer.

---

(3)   You're off to a good start. You remembered the right order of the formula. Now you're ready to learn each step in more detail.

Go on to (4).

---

(4)   S = Survey

The first step toward good study reading is to survey or focus your attention on what you are going to read before you try to read closely. Why? Good question—glad you asked.

The reasons you should survey or preview before reading are:

(1) It will control your attention so that your mind won't wander to other things after reading for a short time, especially if the material is boring.

(2) It prepares you so that you know what the material will be about.

(continued)

(3)   It awakens your subconscious to things you may already know about the subject being read.

(4)   It provides you with an idea of the length of the material to be read and an idea of the time needed to read the assignment.

(5)   It gives you a purpose and direction for reading, a purpose other than the fact the instructor assigned it.

Of course, none of these things mentioned will happen if you don't survey correctly. Before discussing how to survey correctly, check the appropriate box below and then read the designated frame.

I am just a "get-by" student.   ☐   Go to ⑥ .

I am a "super" student.   ☐   Go to ⑤ .

⑤   If you are a super student then you will be interested in not only how to survey an assigned chapter in a textbook but also in how to survey a book. Surveying a book consists of the following steps.

(1)   Read the preface and the introduction. The preface will usually tell you why the author wrote the book, what he will present in it, and for whom the book is intended.

(2)   Read the table of contents. The titles of units and chapters give you a picture of the book's contents.

(3)   Leaf through the book noting what visual aids it may have, such as pictures, graphs, charts, marginal notes, subheadings, and the like. An awareness of these aids will be helpful to you when you read closely.

(4)   Check to see if there are reading lists of reference works and/or a glossary at the end of the book. A glossary can save you many trips to your dictionary.

(5)   If the chapters have summaries, read them quickly. Doing this may take an hour or two, but it is worth it in the long run because you will know what the book covers, what aids it offers you, and you will have a sense of direction for the course the book is being used in.

Now go get a textbook that you are using in one of your classes. No, don't sit there reading this. Go get a textbook.

Good. Now, using the check list on the next page, survey the textbook. Fill in the title and author in the blanks and then place a check mark beside each item your textbook has.

Book title _____   Author _____

☐ 1. Preface

☐ 2. Introduction

☐ 3. Table of Contents

☐ 4. Visual Aids (pictures, graphs, subheadings, comments in the margins, etc.)

☐ 5. Glossary

☐ 6. Index

☐ 7. Chapter Summaries

☐ 8. Other aids not mentioned (specify what): _____

_____

_____

Now let's see if you really are a super student. For each of the items you checked above, read or look more carefully at what the item has to offer. When finished, write a short paragraph in the space below which reflects what you now know about the book that you didn't know before you previewed it.

If you feel that the surveying you have just done doesn't pay off for you by the end of the semester, you can come back to this page and madly mark a big X on it.

Now go on to ⑥ .

(6)   Taking a few minutes to survey a chapter before reading it closely will save time in the long run. It prepares you for what you are
going to read and calls your attention to things you may already
know or don't know about the material. Study carefully Figure A
which shows sample pages from a typical textbook and the types of
aids usually used. Do that now, then come back here.

As you can see, authors use many types of aids to help you prepare to read, to help you organize as you read, and to help you review at a later time. These aids consist of headings, subheadings,
pictures, graphs, capitalized words, italicized words, summaries,
and book lists. But all these aids are only as good as the reader
using them. Learn the following steps for surveying a chapter.

Steps for Surveying a Chapter

(1)   The first thing to do when surveying a chapter is to read
the chapter title and think about what it says or means.

(2)   Next, read the headings and subheadings. Headings not
only reveal the author's organization of material but
also provide you with key phrases which reveal a chapter's basic content. If you know anything about subjects
or have studied them before, the key phrases will trigger
what you have stored in your memory and bring it from
your subconscious to your conscious mind. Subheadings
are breakdowns of main headings. They usually reveal
the important points related to the major heading. The
difference in the size of type or bold print used purposely stands out as a visual aid for the reader.

(3)   The third step is to read the summary if there is one.
A summary will give you all the important points of the
chapter. When you read closely, you will know what is
considered important to remember and you will pay more
attention to those points as they are explained in the
chapter.

(4)   Next, read the captions under the pictures, charts,
graphs, or illustrations. Figure A, which you were
referred to earlier, is an important part of this chapter
and illustrates what is being said now. Looking at such
aids before you read closely puts your head into the
right frame of reference.

(5)   Last, see if there is a bibliography or list of books related to the content of the chapter. You may be required
to do a book report for the class and may need some
idea of what to read.

Bold print heading

List of special points

Sub-headings

Italicized words of importance

Summary

Illustrations

Bibliography with brief descriptions

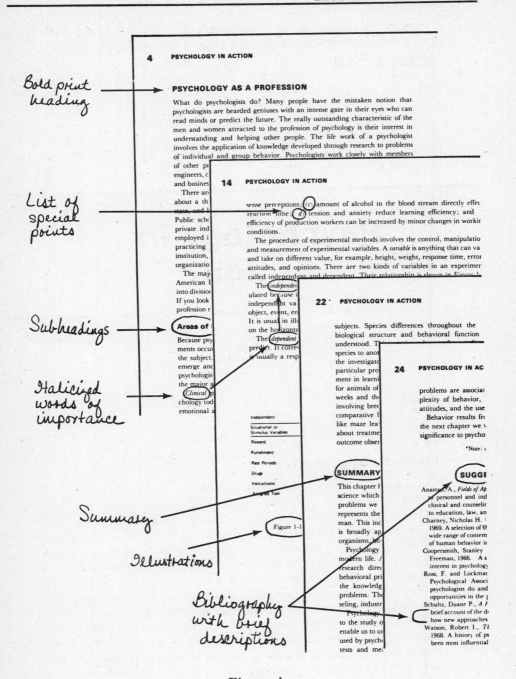

Figure A

Now try each of the five steps listed on page 190, as you survey the following condensed chapter from a textbook, <u>Psychology</u> <u>for</u> <u>a</u> <u>Changing</u> <u>World</u>.

Psychology in Action

WHAT IS PSYCHOLOGY?

Psychology is a subject of increasing interest and concern in our modern complex society. Public awareness has been heightened by movies, television, and the popular press. Although psychology was established as an independent science less than one hundred years ago (1879), its subject matter has been a concern of philosophers and scholars for many centuries. Typical questions for speculation were: What are the functions of the human mind? Where does the mind come from and how does it develop or change? How is mind related to the body? Do animals possess minds? How is mind related to the brain? What is the role of the brain in governing behavior? How do the sense organs and the brain contribute to our perception of the world? How is the soul related to the mind? What causes mental disorders? To what extent is man a product of his culture? How is individual behavior influenced by groups? What are the best methods for raising children? How can we develop and structure the environ-

WHAT IS PSYCHOLOGY   3

ment to make it possible for the inborn potentialities of individuals to be realized? What is human nature and what are its limitations and potentials?

The psychology of today represents a stage in the history of man's inquiry into the nature of man. Prior to the nineteenth century the study of the mind belonged to philosophy, and the study of the body was considered an appropriate subject for anatomy and physiology. The body, as something apart from the mind, was seen as an objective phenomenon, directly observable, and subject to the same general laws that governed other physical matter. The idea of mind and body as separate is no longer considered accurate, although it still persists in popular thought in such expressions as "mind over matter." Both mind and body are combined and interrelated in those expressions of the individual which we call *behavior*. Thoughts, dreams, and wishes, while we cannot see them, are as much a part of an individual, and as expressive of him, as are his acts of walking, talking, or eating. Psychology began as the study of mind, but, as with all branches of modern science, new discoveries and improved methods of inquiry have advanced our understanding of man and the world, until it has evolved into a science of behavior. The term *behavior* is broadly applied to a wide range of activities, including observable action; conscious processes of sensing, feeling, thinking; and unconscious processes within the biological organism which are not directly observable.

Psychology, then, is the study of behavior for the purpose of understanding. We will be examining not only what people do, but also why they do it, what satisfactions or obstacles they find, and why they change. To understand behavior we will need to know something about the physical body—its inherited capacities, how it functions to make behavior possible, its growth and development, and its potentials for change. We will look at the processes of learning which bring changes to behavior as a result of the experiences people have and the training they receive. We will want to know about motives, needs, and wishes that set behavior in motion and propel it forward. Finally, we will look at social and environmental forces that create crises for people and shape their behavior as they make responses to events around them.

Although psychology is a relatively young science, it is rapidly growing in knowledge and expanding its areas of application. The information psychology offers is not limited in its usefulness to just those in the profession. Anyone who comes in contact with people can utilize psychological information to his benefit. Understanding human behavior can help us to do a better job as a student, employee, supervisor, marriage partner, parent, and citizen.

4   PSYCHOLOGY IN ACTION

PSYCHOLOGY AS A PROFESSION

What do psychologists do? Many people have the mistaken notion that psychologists are bearded geniuses with an intense gaze in their eyes who can read minds or predict the future. The really outstanding characteristic of the men and women attracted to the profession of psychology is their interest in understanding and helping other people. The life work of a psychologist involves the application of knowledge developed through research to problems of individual and group behavior. Psychologists work closely with members of other professions including physicians, teachers, lawyers, social workers, engineers, clergymen, nurses, policemen, biochemists, physiologists, sociologists, and business and industrial personnel.

There are approximately thirty thousand psychologists in the United States, about a third of whom are employed by colleges and universities. Federal, state, and local governments make up the second largest group of employers. Public school systems rank third, followed by nonprofit organizations and private industry. There is a growing number of psychologists who are self-employed in therapeutic and consultation activities full time, but most of the practicing psychologists in this country are affiliated with some educational institution, medical facility, governmental agency, or industrial research organization.

The major professional organization for psychologists in this country is the American Psychological Association, founded in 1892. The APA is organized into divisions which represent the major areas of special interest to the members. If you look at the divisions of the APA listed in Table 1-1 you will see that the profession reflects a wide range of interests and application to human problems.

Areas of Specialization

Because psychology has application to all fields of human activity and developments occur so rapidly, psychologists cannot expect to be expert in all areas of the subject. As the profession grows and matures new areas of specialization emerge and develop, although there is still a great deal of overlap in what psychologists do. To give an overview of the profession we will briefly describe the major areas of current specialization.

Clinical psychology is the most popular area of specialization within psychology today. Clinical psychologists engage in the prevention and treatment of emotional and mental disorders (see Chapter 9) by working with individuals

PSYCHOLOGY AS A PROFESSION   **5**

Table 1-1. Divisions of the American Psychological Association[a]

General Psychology
Teaching of Psychology
Experimental Psychology
Evaluation and Measurement
Physiological and Comparative Psychology
Developmental Psychology
Personality and Social Psychology
Society for the Psychological Study of Social Issues
Psychology and the Arts
Clinical Psychology
Consulting Psychology
Industrial Psychology
Educational Psychology
School Psychology
Counseling Psychology
Psychologists in Public Service
Military Psychology
Maturity and Old Age
Society of Engineering Psychologists
Psychological Aspects of Disability
Consumer Psychology
Philosophical Psychology
Experimental Analysis of Behavior
History of Psychology
Community Psychology
Psychopharmacology
Psychotherapy
Psychological Hypnosis
State Psychological Association Affairs

[a]Source: American Psychological Association, 1969.

and small groups who have personal social, emotional, and behavior problems. The clinical psychologist, in addition to training in treatment methods, has special skills in research and the use of psychological testing instruments. The clinical psychologist provides therapy for individuals, families or groups; determines specific behavior problems through interviewing or testing techniques, gives in-service training for other staff members; offers consultations, community education, or organization services; and provides leadership for mental health program development and evaluation. Many clinical psychologists today are involved in community mental health programs aimed at

6   **PSYCHOLOGY IN ACTION**

prevention of illness through better understanding of the causes and improvement of opportunities for healthy development within the community.

Closely related to the clinical field is the specialty of *counseling*. Together these two specialties account for half of all psychologists in our country. Counseling psychologists are primarily concerned with behavior adaptation and the adjustment of individuals to their environment. Counseling psychologists work in vocational guidance, rehabilitation, educational planning, marriage counseling, and community mental health programs. The training and supervision of many elementary and secondary school counselors, classroom teachers, clergymen, law enforcement personnel (especially juvenile workers), and state employment service counselors is a responsibility of counseling psychologists. Both clinical and counseling psychologists are interested in behavior adaptation so that all potentials of the individual may be realized.

Industrial psychologists are the highest paid, on the average, of all psychologists. They comprise about 8 percent of psychologists but they are in increasing demand. They may be employed by industry or government, but frequently they are members of independent groups who sell their services to many different industries. The problems for which industrial psychologists are called upon for service in a given industry may include excessive turnover, absenteeism, inefficiency, or accidents. They may set up a personnel selection and training program to enable a firm to obtain better qualified employees and increase productivity, or help with the selection and appraisal of potential management personnel. Management training courses are frequently offered by industrial psychology firms. Understanding human relations is an important part of industrial management which poses many challenges for the psychologist in industry. Labor–management disputes, poor morale, and breakdown of communication between workers and supervisors are common problems dealt with by the industrial psychologist. Industrial psychologists are also called upon to study complex man–machine systems and to investigate such factors as the arrangement of equipment and work space, designing of tools and equipment, and the prevention of industrial accidents.

Social psychologists study the impact of community and social forces on individual and group behavior and adjustment. Group dynamics, social interaction, delinquency, illegal behavior, and problems of prejudice are among the concerns of the social psychologist. Polling techniques for measuring public opinion, attitudes, and beliefs have become well-known as methods of understanding and predicting group behavior. Some of the newer developments in social psychology include methods for modification of group attitudes to reduce intergroup tension as in congested neighborhoods.

Social psychologists have been increasingly involved in the analysis of propaganda, counterpropaganda, and all aspects of psychological warfare. Social psychology has been applied to business problems with remarkable benefits. Market research includes the testing of products for manufacturers and testing the effectiveness of different advertising techniques in magazines, radio, and television.

Educational psychologists specialize in problems of learning and achievement. They are concerned with the psychological aspects of training, remedial and special education, and school psychology. Recent developments in automated or programmed instruction have attracted many psychologists to this specialty. Research in this new educational technique is still in its infancy, but those who are active in the field are convinced that it will have a dramatic effect upon education in the future.

School psychology has emerged as a separate specialty quite rapidly in the past 20 years. School psychologists usually work in the elementary and secondary schools where they have an opportunity to help children whose problems interfere with their education. The school psychologist emphasizes early detection of learning and behavior problems as the most effective way to prevent later personal and social disability.

Experimental psychology is perhaps one of the least known, but oldest of the special fields of the profession. The experimental psychologist is a research specialist whose efforts to develop theory and make application of newly discovered information has established psychology as a science. The experimentalist works with humans and animals as research subjects and may be found in universities, industry, and government settings. Laboratories for the experimental study of learning, motivation, sensation, perception, and motor skills have become common in the military services and space-age industries. One of the important fields of experimental interest is psychopharmacology, the study of drugs and other chemical agents that produce change in the behavior of living organisms. Working with biochemists, physiologists, and pharmacists, the experimental psychologist conducts research to study the effects of drugs on animals and humans. Psychopharmacology is particularly challenging to the psychologists who work in this area of research because of the potential contributions to be made to the treatment and prevention of human suffering.

8 PSYCHOLOGY IN ACTION

SUMMARY

This chapter has introduced psychology in its perspective as a dynamic modern science which seeks to understand human behavior and help solve the human problems we face in our rapidly changing world. Contemporary psychology represents the current stage in the history of man's inquiry into the nature of man. This inquiry has evolved into a science of behavior. The term behavior is broadly applied to a wide range of activities which characterize living organisms, both animal and human.

Psychology is a rapidly growing profession with many practical applications in modern life. About half of today's psychologists are engaged in teaching and research directed toward increasing our knowledge and understanding of behavioral principles. The other half of the profession is involved in applying the knowledge we now have to the treatment and prevention of human problems. The areas in which psychologists specialize include clinical, counseling, industrial, social, educational, and school psychology.

SUGGESTIONS FOR FURTHER READING

Anastasi, A., *Fields of Applied Psychology*, New York, McGraw-Hill, 1964. An introduction to personnel and industrial psychology, human engineering, consumer psychology, clinical and counseling psychology, and discussion of the contribution of psychology to education, law, and medicine.

Charney, Nicholas H. (Ed.), *Readings in Psychology Today*, Del Mar, Calif., CRM Books, 1969. A selection of 69 articles, with full color illustrations, that is representative of the wide range of contemporary psychological thought, controversial issues, and problems of human behavior in today's world.

Coopersmith, Stanley (Ed.), *Frontiers of Psychological Research*, San Francisco, Calif., Freeman, 1966. A selection of illustrated research reports on topics of contemporary interest in psychology.

Ross, F. and Lockman, R. F., *A Career in Psychology*, Washington, D.C., American Psychological Association, 1963. An illustrated pamphlet that describes what psychologists do and tells where to find out more about the preparation for and opportunities in the profession.

Schultz, Duane P., *A History of Modern Psychology*, New York, Academic Press, 1969. A brief account of the development of psychology in its first century as a science, showing how new approaches to the study of behavior have emerged.

Watson, Robert I., *The Great Psychologists* (2nd ed.), Philadelphia, Pa., Lippincott, 1968. A history of psychology based on the lives and work of the people who have been most influential in its development.

Of course you have not read the chapter—you have only surveyed it—but see how well you can do on these questions. Check what you think are the correct answers.

1. The purpose of the chapter you just surveyed is to show that:

psychology is a rapidly growing profession. ☐ Go to ⑦ .

psychology is a science because it applies a variety of scientific procedures to the study of behavior. ☐ Go to ⑧ .

psychology is a modern science which seeks to understand human behavior and help solve human problems. ☐ Go to ⑨ .

2. The chapter has the following study aids which help explain the chapter's purpose:

headings, subheadings, illustrations, italicized words, summary, and book references. ☐ Go to ⑩ .

headings, subheadings, illustrations, italicized words, summary, study questions. ☐ Go to ⑪ .

---

⑦   Close, but not entirely correct. It is true that your answer is part of the chapter's purpose. The second paragraph of the summary does discuss the point. But if you read the first sentence in the first paragraph of the summary you will see a larger purpose mentioned which includes your answer plus more.

Try another answer in ⑥ .

---

⑧   No deal. It may be true that psychology is a rapidly growing profession, but the purpose of this chapter is to describe it.

Try another answer in ⑥ .

---

⑨   Right you are! Either you lucked out or you used your head. Usually, in a summary the opening statement covers the broad, general statement of purpose with the remaining paragraphs developing more specifically the general statement. From your survey you now know what the chapter will cover.

Now answer question 2 in ⑥ .

---

(10)   Good. You noticed the aids used in the chapter. More will be said about how to use these later. At least now you are aware of what the chapter is about and how it is set up for you to read.

Go to (12) .

---

(11)   Sorry, you goofed. You won't find any study questions in the chapter, only rhetorical questions used in the context of the chapter itself. Look again if you don't believe it.

Then go to (12) .

---

(12)   To show you better how surveying works, go get a textbook that you are using in one of your classes. That's right. Get it now. Put a book marker here until you return. All this will still be here when you get back.

Are you back with the textbook? Good. Using the following check list, survey a chapter from the book which you have not read yet, preferably one you have been assigned to read. Fill in the title of the chapter and place a check mark beside each item the book has.

Chapter title _____

☐	1. Headings
☐	2. Subheadings
☐	3. Summary
☐	4. Pictures
☐	5. Graphs and charts
☐	6. Other illustrations
☐	7. Bibliography
☐	8. Other aids not mentioned (specify what): _____

_____

_____

In the space provided at the top of the next page, write a short paragraph which reflects what you now know about the chapter that you didn't know before.

If, after surveying this chapter, your comprehension and concentration isn't improved when you read the chapter closely, you have permission to call the author of this book nasty names.

Before going on to the next step of the SQ3R study-reading formula, let's check to see how well you understand the surveying process.

If you are a "super" student, go to (13) .

If you are a "get-by" student, go to (14) .

---

(13)   Hi Superstud(ent). In the blank spaces below, write the steps for surveying a <u>textbook</u> in the proper order.

1. _____

2. _____

3. _____

4. _____

5. _____

Check your answers in (15) .

---

(14)   In the blank spaces below, write the steps for surveying a <u>chapter</u> in the proper order.

1. _____

2. _____

3. _____

4. _____

5. _____   (continued)

Check your answers in (16).

---

(15) You should have listed the following steps for surveying a textbook.

1. Read the preface and introduction.
2. Read the table of contents.
3. Check for visual aids.
4. Check for reference works and glossaries.
5. Read the summaries.

If you were correct, go to (14).

If you missed any one of these or missed the order, return to (5) and read it again.

When you understand the order, go to (14).

---

(16) You should have listed the following steps for surveying a chapter.

1. Read the title and let it "sink" in.
2. Read the headings and subheadings.
3. Read the summary.
4. Read the captions.
5. Check for a bibliography.

If you were correct, go to (18).

If you missed any one of these or missed the order, return to (6) and read it again.

When you understand the order, go to (18).

---

(17) What are you doing here? There were no directions sending you here. Scat! Go back to the last frame you read and find out where you belong.

---

(18) Q = Question

The second step of the SQ3R study-reading formula is question. You probably know already that we can remember something much better if it has some specific meaning for us. That's why reading an assigned chapter from a textbook simply because the instructor said to read it is not always a meaningful experience. If you have no real purpose for reading something—other than that it was assigned—you will get little meaningful comprehension.

Purpose in reading is discussed in the other chapters of this book because of its importance to good comprehension and rate adjustment. Study reading, usually thought of as slow, plodding, mind-wandering type reading, need not be that way. In fact, just as in skimming and scanning (techniques discussed in Chapter 2), if you know what you are looking for you can read faster with no mind wandering and better comprehension of your textbook reading assignment.

The best way to get more from reading assignments is to ask yourself questions about what you are going to read. Questions aid study reading because they focus attention on the subject matter. They provide a personal purpose for reading—a purpose beyond the fact the material is assigned. Looking for answers to questions also keeps the mind from wandering to other things as we read and therefore speeds up the studying process.

Surveying, if done properly, provides a natural setting for asking questions. Here are some examples of the kinds of questions you might ask yourself while surveying or after surveying. Learn them; they are important.

(1) What does the title of the chapter mean?

(2) What do I already know about the subject?

(3) What did my instructor say about this chapter or subject when it was assigned? (He may have said something in class or on a handout sheet.)

(4) What questions do the headings and subheadings suggest? (Some study-skills experts recommend that you turn the chapter title and headings into questions.) For example, you might have asked when you started reading this section, "What does Q = Question mean?"

(5) Are there questions at the beginning or end of the chapter? (These questions are often skipped by students when they should be read carefully since they ask what the author obviously thinks is important.)

(6) Are there questions in the workbook that may go with the textbook? (Often workbooks accompany textbooks and contain questions related to the chapter assigned. Make good use of such aids.)

(7) What do I want to know about the contents of this chapter when I am finished reading?

(continued)

Now look over the questions once again and make certain you know them and understand them.

Go to ⑲ .

---

⑲ Practice is what makes a skill perfect—provided it's the right kind of practice. So, once again it is time to practice what you just learned. Turn back to the sample chapter from a psychology textbook you surveyed, on pages 192-198. Pretend you have to read the chapter for a psychology class that you are taking. This time follow the steps for surveying and questioning together. Right now, you are only preparing to read it. You will notice that not all of the sample questions listed in ⑱ can be applied to this "pretend" assignment, but at least see what kinds of questions you can come up with.

Ready? Back to the sample chapter and try what you just learned. Then come back here.

Fine. Now check your technique by turning the following headings from the chapter into questions that could guide your reading. In the space provided, write what you think is a good question to ask yourself while reading that section in the chapter.

1. "Psychology in Action" (the title of the chapter)

_____

2. "What is Psychology?"

_____

3. "Psychology As A Profession"

_____

4. "Areas of Specialization"

_____

Check your answers with these. The wording may be different but the ideas should be close.

1. "What does 'psychology in action' mean?" "How can psychology be active?"
2. "What is psychology?" The heading is already a question.
3. "Is psychology a profession?" or "Why is psychology called a profession if it is a science?"
4. "What areas of specialization are there?"

If you had these questions or ones like them, go to (20) .

If you had trouble understanding what was meant by Q = Question, read (18) again and pay attention to the way the questions listed came from the headings in the sample psychology textbook chapter. Then go to (20) .

---

(20)   Is that textbook you were using before still near? Get it again, please. Then open it to the chapter you surveyed and answer each of the following questions in the spaces provided.

Title of book _____ Author _____

Title of chapter _____

1. What does the title of the chapter mean?

_____

_____

2. What do I already know about the subject?

a. _____

b. _____

c. _____

3. What did my instructor say about this chapter or subject when it was assigned?

_____

_____

4. What questions do the headings and subheadings suggest?

a. _____

b. _____

c. _____

5. Are there questions at the beginning or end of the chapter?

_____ Did you read them? _____

6. Are there questions in the workbook? (This may not apply to your book.) _____ Did you read them? _____

(continued)

7. What do I want to know about the contents of this chapter when I am finished reading?

a. _____

b. _____

c. _____

What you just did probably seemed like a time consuming job. Remember, however, that while you were asked to do this in writing now, you will be doing this mentally as you survey. Right now these steps may take more time than they will later, but that's because you are in the process of learning. The actual time it takes to survey and question is really a matter of minutes. These few minutes will be well worth the better comprehension you will receive in the long run.

Go to (21) .

---

(21)   Here's a quick review before going to the next step of the SQ3R method.

A. SQ3R stands for (fill in the blanks):

S _____

Q _____

R^1 _____

R^2 _____

R^3 _____

Turn to (22) for the answer.

B. List the five steps for surveying a <u>chapter</u>.

1. _____

2. _____

3. _____

4. _____

5. _____

Turn to (23) for the answer.

C. List the types of <u>questions</u> you should ask yourself as you survey.

1. _____

2. _____

3. _____

4. _____

5. _____

6. _____

7. _____

Turn to ㉔ and check your answers.

㉒ Survey, Question, Read, Recite, Review

If you were correct, pat yourself on the back and then answer question B in ㉑ .

If you missed any one of these steps, return to page 186 and re-read the explanation. It is important that you memorize the correct order of the SQ3R formula. Then answer question B in ㉑ .

㉓ Your answers should be in the following order.

1. Read the title and let it "sink" in.
2. Read the headings and subheadings.
3. Read the summary.
4. Read the captions.
5. Check for a bibliography.

If you were correct, smile loudly and go to question C in ㉑ .

If you missed any part of the question, return to ⑥ and read the section <u>Steps</u> <u>for</u> <u>Surveying</u> <u>a</u> <u>Chapter</u>. Learn those five points well. Then answer question C in ㉑ .

Your answers should be in the following order.

1. What does the title of the chapter mean?
2. What do I already know about the subject?
3. What did my instructor say about the chapter when it was assigned?
4. What questions do the headings and subheadings suggest?
5. Are there questions at the beginning or end of the chapter?
6. Are there questions in an accompanying workbook?
7. What do I want to know about the contents of the chapter when I am finished?

If you answered all of these correctly, sigh in relief and go to .

If you goofed, return to (18) and read it again.

When you can correctly answer question C, go to (25) .

 $\underline{R^1 = Read}$

The third step of the SQ3R formula is to read. Too many students begin reading an assignment without any preparations such as the survey and question steps. The results usually are poor comprehension, mind wandering, and lots of rereading of parts that don't make sense. It is true that your assignment is to be read, but not without the proper preparation that the S and Q techniques offer. The actual close reading of the material will be easier and comprehension will be better after you have prepared.

Here is how you should do your close reading ($\underline{R^1 = Read}$). Learn these steps. They are important to remember.

(1) Read to answer the questions you raised while doing the survey/question routine; or read to answer the questions at the beginning or end of the chapter if there are any. Remember, reading to answer these questions gives you a purpose and a sense of direction.

(2) Read all the added attractions in the chapter. Most textbooks have pictures, maps, graphs, tables, and other illustrations which supplement or clarify what the author is saying.

(3) Read extra carefully all the underlined, italicized, or bold printed words or phrases. When terms are printed in different size type, it means the author is calling attention to them. Study such terms carefully. Usually they are quiz or test items.

Read the three points again. Make certain you know them.

Now return to the sample textbook chapter on psychology in (6).

You have already applied the survey/question techniques, but you may want to S/Q again. This time apply step three, R^1 = Read, looking for answers to questions you raised.

When you have finished, go to (26).

---

(26)   If you have finished using R^1 = Read on the sample chapter, answer the following questions so you can see how well you read. Check the appropriate answer.

Question 1. According to the chapter you read, psychology is defined as:

man's inquiry into the nature of man.   ☐ See (27).

the study of behavior for the purpose of
understanding.   ☐ See (28).

don't know.   ☐ See (29).

---

(27)   If you selected this answer, you misread somewhere. If you look at the second paragraph of the chapter you'll notice it states: "The psychology of today represents a stage in the history of man's inquiry into the nature of man." Notice the words a stage in the history of man's inquiry. This is not a definition, but a statement about the position of psychology in the history of man.

Go back to (26) and read the other answer, then go to (28).

---

(28)   You're right there! After all the discussion about psychology, it is finally defined in the third paragraph of the chapter. The title of the first heading is "What is Psychology?" and you apparently looked for an answer to this question. Good work.

Now try Question 2 in (30).

---

(29)   At least you're honest. Read the third paragraph under "What is Psychology?" and try again.

---

(30) Question 2. About how many of today's psychologists are engaged in teaching and research?

one-third □ See (31) .

about half □ See (32) .

(31) You missed this when you shouldn't have. The Summary tells you the amount. Did you read the Summary when you surveyed? The second paragraph of the Summary tells you that one-half are employed in teaching and research. Read the second paragraph of the Summary again.

Then go to (33) .

(32) Good—if you didn't guess. If you did, check out the second paragraph of the Summary.

Go on to (33) .

(33) Question 3. The purpose of Table 1-1 in the sample chapter is:

to show how many areas of specialization in psychology exist. □ See (34) .

to provide information about the American Psychological Association. □ See (35) .

there is no table in the chapter. □ See (36) .

(34) You're so smart! Go on to Question 4 in (37) .

(35) Negative. It's true the information in the table is from that source, but the use of the list is to illustrate the whole point of the subheading "Areas of Specialization."

Try another answer in (33) .

(36) Are you kidding? What were you thinking about when you read? If you didn't know there was a table in the chapter after surveying, questioning, and reading, you'd better check to see if someone has

been giving you a hot foot without your feeling it. Let's try again.

Look at that sample chapter again, then return to ㉝ and answer Question 3.

㊲ Question 4. How many areas of specialization in which psychologists specialize were discussed?

six	☐	See ㊳.
seven	☐	See ㊴.
I did not notice any specific number.	☐	See ㊵.

㊳ Six, you say? Wrong you are. What were you doing, guessing? Well, maybe you counted wrong. Under the subheading "Areas of Specialization" you will find several paragraphs discussing these special areas. Each paragraph begins with an italicized word. Remember the steps for R^1 = Read? Pay close attention to italicized words or terms. They are usually test items. Go back and count them. Then reread the last paragraph in the Summary and ask yourself what you were thinking about when you read. It wasn't what you should have been thinking about.

Try another answer in ㊲.

㊴ Good. You must have noted each of the seven areas were italicized to call your attention to them. Or maybe you remembered from reading the Summary.

Go on to ㊶.

㊵ Hmm. True, the areas of specialization were not listed by number, but they were pointed out to you twice, under "Areas of Specialization" and in the Summary. Look again at the chapter.

Try another answer in ㊲.

㊶ Once more, get that textbook you have been practicing with. Select a chapter you have not read yet and practice using the survey/question technique. On the next page, answer the questions about the chapter.

(continued)

1. Chapter title _____

2. What are some questions the title raises or that you want answered?

   a. _____

   b. _____

   c. _____

3. What subjects do the headings deal with?

   a. _____

   b. _____

   c. _____

4. What do you already know about these subjects?

   a. _____

   b. _____

   c. _____

5. What do you want to know when you finish reading this chapter?

   a. _____

   b. _____

   c. _____

Now read the chapter from your textbook following the three points mentioned under $\underline{R^1} = \underline{Read}$. Then return here.

If you are finished reading the chapter from your textbook, answer the following questions.

6. Write the answers to the questions you wrote down under number 2 above.

   a. _____

   b. _____

   c. _____

7. Write down one thing you learned about each of the subjects you wrote down under number 3.

   a. _____

   b. _____

   c. _____

8.   Did you find answers for each point you listed under number 5?

a.   _____

b.   _____

c.   _____

I can't help you with your answers, but at least I helped you to apply what you are learning in this book to an actual textbook for one of your classes. Remember to keep trying these methods on your actual assignments.

Now go on to (42).

R^2 = Recite

The fourth step of the SQ3R study formula is <u>recite</u>. For the purposes of this formula, recite means to go over what you read in step three (R^1 = Read) by either orally summarizing what you just read, or by making notes of some type. Studies reveal that students tend to forget as much as 80 percent of what they learned from reading within two weeks after studying. On the other hand, when students recited immediately after reading, they forgot only 20 percent during the same time period. It is a known fact that recitation reinforces what you read, helps you to see what mistakes you may have made when you read it the first time.

Here are a few "don'ts" when you do the R^2 = Recite step.

(1)   Don't stop to recite after every paragraph or two. This will break the continuity of the section you are reading.

(2)   Don't wait to recite if a section from one heading to another is too long. You should use your own judgment about places to stop and recite.

(3)   Don't underline long passages. It is better to be selective and mark only key ideas or terms.

(4)   Don't use ink to mark your book unless you don't make mistakes. You can erase pencil marks.

(5)   Don't underline or mark as you read; mark only <u>after</u> you have read the passage and understand it.

If you follow this advice, you will find your marks are more meaningful when you review for a test weeks or months later.

(continued)

Return now to that old familiar sample chapter from a psychology test in ⑥ . You applied $\underline{R^1} = \underline{Read}$ to it already. This time return to the subheading "Areas of Specialization" and apply $\underline{R^2} = \underline{Recite}$ to it. Then return here again.

If you forgot or neglected to orally recite after reading, see ㊸ .

If you remembered to recite orally, write a summary in the space below of what you orally recited when you finished the section "Areas of Specialization."

Now go to ㊹ and compare your summary with it.

㊸ Shame on you. How are you going to be a better student if you don't try what you are learning? Go back to ㊷ and in your own words orally recite what you think the section was about. Then in the space provided in ㊷ write a summary of your recitation.

㊹ Compare your summary with this one. Naturally, wording will be different but the main ideas should be contained in your summary. Key words and phrases are underlined.

The field of psychology has <u>seven</u> major <u>areas of specialization</u>. (1) <u>Clinical psychology</u>, the <u>most popular</u> area, deals with the <u>prevention</u> and <u>treatment</u> of emotional and mental disorders. (2) <u>Counseling</u>, along with the clinical field, accounts for <u>over half of all psychiatrists</u> in the U.S. This branch is concerned with <u>behavior</u> and <u>adjustment</u>. (3) The third group, <u>industrial</u> psychologists, are the <u>highest paid</u>. They deal with <u>personnel</u> and <u>management</u> problems. (4) <u>Social</u> psychologists study the impact of <u>social forces</u> on individual and group behavior.

(5) <u>Educational</u> psychologists specialize in <u>learning</u> <u>and</u> <u>achievement</u>. (6) <u>School</u> psychologists work with students whose <u>problems</u> <u>interfere</u> <u>with</u> <u>their</u> <u>education</u>. (7) <u>Experimental</u> psychologists deal primarily with <u>research</u> <u>projects</u>.

Make certain your summary covers all seven areas and defines what these areas are. If your summary does not contain these elements, go to ⑤ . If your summary compares well, go to ㊻ .

---

⑤ You might have had trouble with your summary because you were not paying attention to the clues given you in the chapter. The subhead "Areas of Specialization" should raise the question, "What <u>are</u> the areas of specialization?" As you read to find the answer, you should have noticed that each one is an italicized term. Skim over the section "Areas of Specialization" again and fill in the following blanks. The first one has been done for you.

	Area	Job Description
1.	*clinical*	*treatment of mental disorders*
2.	_____	_____
3.	_____	_____
4.	_____	_____
5.	_____	_____
6.	_____	_____
7.	_____	_____

Compare your answers with these.

2. counseling   behavior and adjustment adaptation
3. industrial   personnel and management problems
4. social   reaction to social forces of individual and group behavior
5. educational   learning and achievement
6. school   students' problems
7. experimental   research projects

If you missed any of these, reread the paragraph dealing with the particular area of specialization you missed.

If you got all of these correct, go on to ㊻ .

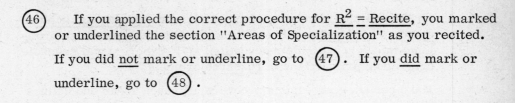

(46)   If you applied the correct procedure for R^2 = Recite, you marked or underlined the section "Areas of Specialization" as you recited. If you did not mark or underline, go to (47) . If you did mark or underline, go to (48) .

(47)   Are you stubborn or did you forget to mark and underline as you recited? Why don't you go back to (42) and start all over. This time, pay attention to the steps involved in R^2 = Recite and the reasons for them.

(48)   There is not enough space in this book to give you sample markings for comparison of the entire section you marked. However, Figure B is a one-page reproduction of part of the section you marked. Compare your markings with Figure B. Notice the following points.

    (1)   The page has not been over-marked.
    (2)   Numbers are used in the margin to designate new areas of specialization being discussed.
    (3)   Key phrases are circled; detailed points are underlined.
    (4)   Points needed for a quick review before a test are all marked for special attention.
    (5)   A brief summary is written at the end of the section.

If you did not mark as shown in Figure B, reread the steps for R^2 = Recite again and also study Figure B carefully.

If your markings look like mine, go on to (49) .

(49) R^3 = Review

The fifth and last step of the SQ3R study formula is to review. Most students do review what they have read just before taking a test. But there is more to it than that. Reviewing should combine the use of the total SQ3R formula. It consists of surveying what you have read again, only this time you already know what the material is; and you are surveying to see what you remember about the title, headings, and subheadings. It also consists of using your notes or markings to refresh your memory regarding the key points you already found when you read and recited.

4. (cont)
social psychology include methods for modification of group attitudes to reduce intergroup tension as in congested neighborhoods.

Social psychologists have been increasingly involved in the analysis of propaganda, counterpropaganda, and all aspects of psychological warfare. Social psychology has been applied to business problems with remarkable benefits. Market research includes the testing of products for manufacturers and testing the effectiveness of different advertising techniques in magazines, radio, and television.

5. Educational psychologists specialize in problems of learning and achievement. They are concerned with the psychological aspects of training, remedial and special education, and school psychology. Recent developments in automated or programmed instruction have attracted many psychologists to this specialty. Research in this new educational technique is still in its infancy, but those who are active in the field are convinced that it will have a dramatic effect upon education in the future.

6. School psychology has emerged as a separate specialty quite rapidly in the past 20 years. School psychologists usually work in the elementary and secondary schools where they have an opportunity to help children whose problems interfere with their education. The school psychologist emphasizes early detection of learning and behavior problems as the most effective way to prevent later personal and social disability.

7. Experimental psychology is perhaps one of the least known, but oldest of the special fields of the profession. The experimental psychologist is a research specialist whose efforts to develop theory and make application of newly discovered information has established psychology as a science. The experimentalist works with humans and animals as research subjects and may be found in universities, industry, and government settings. Laboratories for the experimental study of learning, motivation, sensation, perception, and motor skills have become common in the military services and space-age industries. One of the important fields of experimental interest is psychopharmacology, the study of drugs and other chemical agents that produce change in the behavior of living organisms. Working with biochemists, physiologists, and pharmacists, the experimental psychologist conducts research to study the effects of drugs on animals and humans. Psychopharmacology is particularly challenging to the psychologists who work in this area of research because of the potential contributions to be made to the treatment and prevention of human suffering.

Seven major areas of specialization: clinical, counseling, industrial, social, educational, school, experimental.

Figure B

Here are the proper steps for R^3 = Review. Learn them.

(1) Review immediately after reading a chapter. This means reading over your notes or markings and putting together all the different sections of the chapter so you have a total picture of what you read. This immediate review will be fairly short because everything will be fresh in your mind.

(2) Review periodically. After you have read other chapters and a few weeks have passed, go back and review earlier chapters so that you can get a picture of the progress the textbook is making.

(3) Plan a final review before taking an exam on the subject. Plan ahead so that you have time to do a careful, thorough review.

If you are a "get-by" student, go to ⑤⓪ .

If you are a "super" student, go to ⑤① .

⸻

⑤⓪   About all we can say now is try the SQ3R system on some of your textbooks. Take what you've learned here and use it. Books vary, so feel free to "bend" the formula and the steps in it to fit your particular book. Thousands of students have pulled up their grades by using the SQ3R formula. When you first use it, you may find yourself concentrating too much on how to use it, rather than on what you are reading. Don't worry about it and don't blame the formula. A little practice and you will be using the formula steps without thinking about them. That's when you'll feel the difference. Good luck!

Go to ⑤② .

⸻

⑤①   Glad to have you back. Here's a chance for you to see if all you have been learning really pays off. Once again, return to the sample psychology chapter and review it. Then answer the following questions about the chapter. Circle the correct true/false response.

T / F 1. Psychology is the study of behavior for the purpose of understanding.

T / F 2. Both mind and body are combined and interrelated in those expressions of the individual which are called behavior.

T / F 3. Psychology is a relatively young science.

T / F 4. The major professional organization for psychologists in this country is the American Psychological Association.

T / F 5. Clinical psychology is the second most popular area of specialization within psychology today.

T / F 6. The problems industrial psychologists concern themselves with are often absenteeism, inefficiency, accidents, and employee turnover.

T / F 7. There are eight major areas of specialization in the field of psychology.

T / F 8. Contemporary psychology represents the current stage in the history of man's inquiry into the nature of man.

Compare your answers with these: 1. T; 2. T; 3. T; 4. T; 5. F (it's the first); 6. T; 7. F (there are seven); 8. T.

Chances are you got at least six of the eight questions or more. If you had trouble, don't worry too much about it at this point. After all, this is not a psychology course! However, the majority of the students who tried this material before it got into print scored six or better. For those questions you missed, you might want to skim back and see where you goofed.

Go back to 50 now.

---

52 Many students cram before an exam. Sometimes the results are good—for that particular test. However, most often the results of cramming are disastrous. I don't recommend it. But if you are going to cram, at least use part of the SQ3R formula we've been dealing with so far—R^2 = Recite. Assuming you have read the chapters you are to be tested on, it will be to your advantage to get together with a friend or two and orally recite to one another. Try these steps.

(1) Ask each other what the titles of chapters really mean.

(2) Ask each other to explain what the headings and subheadings in the chapter mean.

(3) Ask each other to define italicized or bold print words or terms.

(continued)

(4) Ask each other questions based on tables, charts, pictures, etc., in the chapters.

(5) Ask each other what types of questions you think the instructor will ask on the test.

(6) If there are questions at the end of the chapters, or if the instructor gave out a handout sheet with questions, try answering them in your own words.

(7) Don't wait until the last minute to do your cramming. Get a good night's rest.

Recitation helps you organize your thoughts, forces you to put your thoughts into words, and helps you remember things longer. But a one-shot cramming scene before a test will tend to confuse you and jam up your mind. If you do cram and pass the test, chances are you will forget it all in a matter of days or even hours. If that's the type of education you want, you're welcome to it.

This ends the chapter on improving study reading.

In order to help you develop your SQ3R technique, use the following practice pages on your textbooks.

PRACTICE PAGES FOR
SURVEYING A <u>TEXTBOOK</u>

There are five worksheets, all the same, on the following pages. Use
them in the manner outlined below.

(1) Select a textbook you are currently using in a class.

(2) Tear one of the following worksheets from this book.

(3) Answer the questions on the worksheet by using the text
you selected.

(4) Do the same for the remaining worksheets.

(5) Follow the same routine on your own even after the worksheets are used up.

Surveying Your Textbook

1. Name of textbook. _____

2. List at least three questions or thoughts which the title suggests to you.

    a. _____

    b. _____

    c. _____

3. List at least two major points the author makes in the Preface.

    a. _____

    b. _____

4. List at least two major points the author makes in his Introduction.

    a. _____

    b. _____

5. Take at least five chapter titles listed in the Table of Contents and turn them into questions.

    a. _____

    b. _____

    c. _____

    d. _____

    e. _____

6. If there is an Appendix, what does it contain?

    _____

    _____

    _____

7. Does the book contain a Glossary? _____ An Index? _____
   If the answers are yes, look over the Glossary and/or thumb through the Index, looking for familiar names, places, or terms. How much do you think you are going to know about the contents?

    _____

    _____

8. Look through the first two chapters of the book and check any of the following aids used in them.

____ headings	____ study questions
____ subheadings	____ assignments
____ italics	____ graphs, charts
____ summary	____ pictures
____ footnotes	____ other: _____
____ bibliography	

9. Write a short statement regarding your hopes, fears, expectations, etc., about the book.

Surveying Your Textbook

1. Name of textbook. _____

2. List at least three questions or thoughts which the title suggests to you.

   a. _____

   b. _____

   c. _____

3. List at least two major points the author makes in the Preface.

   a. _____

   b. _____

4. List at least two major points the author makes in his Introduction.

   a. _____

   b. _____

5. Take at least five chapter titles listed in the Table of Contents and turn them into questions.

   a. _____

   b. _____

   c. _____

   d. _____

   e. _____

6. If there is an Appendix, what does it contain?

   _____

   _____

7. Does the book contain a Glossary? _____ An Index? _____
   If the answers are yes, look over the Glossary and/or thumb through the Index, looking for familiar names, places, or terms. How much do you think you are going to know about the contents?

   _____

   _____

8. Look through the first two chapters of the book and check any of the following aids used in them.

_____ headings   _____ study questions
_____ subheadings   _____ assignments
_____ italics   _____ graphs, charts
_____ summary   _____ pictures
_____ footnotes   _____ other: _____
_____ bibliography

9. Write a short statement regarding your hopes, fears, expectations, etc., about the book.

Surveying Your Textbook

1. Name of textbook. _____

2. List at least three questions or thoughts which the title suggests to you.

    a. _____

    b. _____

    c. _____

3. List at least two major points the author makes in the Preface.

    a. _____

    b. _____

4. List at least two major points the author makes in his Introduction.

    a. _____

    b. _____

5. Take at least five chapter titles listed in the Table of Contents and turn them into questions.

    a. _____

    b. _____

    c. _____

    d. _____

    e. _____

6. If there is an Appendix, what does it contain?

    _____

    _____

    _____

7. Does the book contain a Glossary? _____ An Index? _____
    If the answers are yes, look over the Glossary and/or thumb through the Index, looking for familiar names, places, or terms. How much do you think you are going to know about the contents?

    _____

    _____

8. Look through the first two chapters of the book and check any of the
    following aids used in them.

    _____ headings   _____ study questions
    _____ subheadings   _____ assignments
    _____ italics   _____ graphs, charts
    _____ summary   _____ pictures
    _____ footnotes   _____ other: _____
    _____ bibliography

9. Write a short statement regarding your hopes, fears, expectations,
    etc., about the book.

Surveying Your Textbook

1. Name of textbook. _____

2. List at least three questions or thoughts which the title suggests to you.

   a. _____

   b. _____

   c. _____

3. List at least two major points the author makes in the Preface.

   a. _____

   b. _____

4. List at least two major points the author makes in his Introduction.

   a. _____

   b. _____

5. Take at least five chapter titles listed in the Table of Contents and turn them into questions.

   a. _____

   b. _____

   c. _____

   d. _____

   e. _____

6. If there is an Appendix, what does it contain?

   _____

   _____

7. Does the book contain a Glossary? _____ An Index? _____
   If the answers are yes, look over the Glossary and/or thumb through the Index, looking for familiar names, places, or terms. How much do you think you are going to know about the contents?

   _____

   _____

8. Look through the first two chapters of the book and check any of the following aids used in them.

_____	headings	_____	study questions
_____	subheadings	_____	assignments
_____	italics	_____	graphs, charts
_____	summary	_____	pictures
_____	footnotes	_____	other: _____
_____	bibliography		

9. Write a short statement regarding your hopes, fears, expectations, etc., about the book.

Surveying Your Textbook

1. Name of textbook. _____

2. List at least three questions or thoughts which the title suggests to you.

   a. _____

   b. _____

   c. _____

3. List at least two major points the author makes in the Preface.

   a. _____

   b. _____

4. List at least two major points the author makes in his Introduction.

   a. _____

   b. _____

5. Take at least five chapter titles listed in the Table of Contents and turn them into questions.

   a. _____

   b. _____

   c. _____

   d. _____

   e. _____

6. If there is an Appendix, what does it contain?

   _____

   _____

   _____

7. Does the book contain a Glossary? _____ An Index? _____
   If the answers are yes, look over the Glossary and/or thumb through the Index, looking for familiar names, places, or terms. How much do you think you are going to know about the contents?

   _____

   _____

8. Look through the first two chapters of the book and check any of the following aids used in them.

_____ headings	_____ study questions
_____ subheadings	_____ assignments
_____ italics	_____ graphs, charts
_____ summary	_____ pictures
_____ footnotes	_____ other: _____
_____ bibliography	

9. Write a short statement regarding your hopes, fears, expectations, etc., about the book.

PRACTICE PAGES FOR SURVEYING
A <u>TEXTBOOK</u> <u>CHAPTER</u>

There are five worksheets on the following pages.   Use them in the
manner outlined below.

(1)   Select a textbook you are using in a class you are taking,
preferably a book which you are having trouble reading.

(2)   Tear one of the following worksheets from this book.

(3)   Answer the questions on the worksheet by using a chapter
you have not read in the book you have selected.

(4)   Do the same for the remaining worksheets.

(5)   Follow the same routine on other chapters even after the
worksheets are used up.

Surveying a Textbook Chapter

1. Name of the textbook. _____

2. Chapter title. _____

3. List at least three questions the title suggests to you.

    a. _____

    b. _____

    c. _____

4. Read the first paragraph, each bold heading and subheading, and the last two paragraphs of the chapter. What is the chapter about?

    _____

    _____

    _____

5. How much do you already know about the subject?

    _____

    _____

6. What study aids does the chapter contain?

    _____ bold print   _____ summary
    _____ italicized words   _____ bibliography
    _____ graphs, charts, etc.   _____ questions
    _____ pictures   _____ other: _____

7. How long will it take you to study this chapter? _____

8. If you will need to divide the chapter up into sections to study it, where are you going to divide it? (Name page numbers.)

    _____

9. List at least four questions you are going to read to find answers to.

    a. _____

    b. _____

    c. _____

    d. _____

Surveying a Textbook Chapter

1. Name of the textbook. _____

2. Chapter title. _____

3. List at least three questions the title suggests to you.

   a. _____

   b. _____

   c. _____

4. Read the first paragraph, each bold heading and subheading, and the last two paragraphs of the chapter. What is the chapter about?

   _____

   _____

   _____

5. How much do you already know about the subject?

   _____

   _____

6. What study aids does the chapter contain?

   ____ bold print   ____ summary
   ____ italicized words   ____ bibliography
   ____ graphs, charts, etc. ____ questions
   ____ pictures   ____ other: _____

7. How long will it take you to study this chapter? _____

8. If you will need to divide the chapter up into sections to study it, where are you going to divide it? (Name page numbers.)

   _____

9. List at least four questions you are going to read to find answers to.

   a. _____

   b. _____

   c. _____

   d. _____

Surveying a Textbook Chapter

1. Name of the textbook. _____

2. Chapter title. _____

3. List at least three questions the title suggests to you.

    a. _____

    b. _____

    c. _____

4. Read the first paragraph, each bold heading and subheading, and the last two paragraphs of the chapter. What is the chapter about?

    _____

    _____

    _____

5. How much do you already know about the subject?

    _____

    _____

6. What study aids does the chapter contain?

    ____ bold print   ____ summary
    ____ italicized words   ____ bibliography
    ____ graphs, charts, etc. ____ questions
    ____ pictures   ____ other: _____

7. How long will it take you to study this chapter? _____

8. If you will need to divide the chapter up into sections to study it, where are you going to divide it? (Name page numbers.)

    _____

9. List at least four questions you are going to read to find answers to.

    a. _____

    b. _____

    c. _____

    d. _____

Surveying a Textbook Chapter

1. Name of the textbook. _____

2. Chapter title. _____

3. List at least three questions the title suggests to you.

    a. _____

    b. _____

    c. _____

4. Read the first paragraph, each bold heading and subheading, and the last two paragraphs of the chapter. What is the chapter about?

    _____

    _____

    _____

5. How much do you already know about the subject?

    _____

    _____

6. What study aids does the chapter contain?

    ____ bold print   ____ summary
    ____ italicized words   ____ bibliography
    ____ graphs, charts, etc.   ____ questions
    ____ pictures   ____ other: _____

7. How long will it take you to study this chapter? _____

8. If you will need to divide the chapter up into sections to study it, where are you going to divide it? (Name page numbers.)

    _____

9. List at least four questions you are going to read to find answers to.

    a. _____

    b. _____

    c. _____

    d. _____

Surveying a Textbook Chapter

1. Name of the textbook. _____

2. Chapter title. _____

3. List at least three questions the title suggests to you.

   a. _____

   b. _____

   c. _____

4. Read the first paragraph, each bold heading and subheading, and the last two paragraphs of the chapter. What is the chapter about?

   _____

   _____

   _____

5. How much do you already know about the subject?

   _____

   _____

6. What study aids does the chapter contain?

   ____ bold print   ____ summary
   ____ italicized words   ____ bibliography
   ____ graphs, charts, etc.   ____ questions
   ____ pictures   ____ other: _____

7. How long will it take you to study this chapter? _____

8. If you will need to divide the chapter up into sections to study it, where are you going to divide it? (Name page numbers.)

   _____

9. List at least four questions you are going to read to find answers to.

   a. _____

   b. _____

   c. _____

   d. _____

Index